SCIENTIFIC KENTUCKY

DUANE S. NICKELL

THE
History
PRESS

Published by The History Press
Charleston, SC
www.historypress.com

Copyright © 2022 by Duane S. Nickell
All rights reserved

Opposite: *Shutterstock*.

First published 2022

Manufactured in the United States

ISBN 9781540252746

Library of Congress Control Number: 2022935426

To my Kentucky family and friends.
May the sun continue to shine bright on y'all.

CONTENTS

ACKNOWLEDGEMENTS

I was born and raised in Kentucky, and although I now live in Indiana, I still cry when I hear "My Old Kentucky Home." I want to thank all the people of Kentucky who were a part of my life. I am especially grateful that I had a mother, Anna June Nickell, and a father, Carl Duane "Red" Nickell, who read to me every night and filled my home with books. Thanks also to all the teachers of the Paducah Public Schools who contributed to my education. Thanks to my editor, Chad Rhoad, for his assistance in guiding me through the process of getting this book published. And thanks to the team at The History Press for their help in polishing the manuscript and designing the cover. Most of all, I want to thank my wife, Karen Markman, for her careful reading, critiquing and editing of my work.

INTRODUCTION

When you think of Kentucky, what words come to mind? Basketball, bluegrass, bourbon and horses, right? The word science probably doesn't occur to you. When you think of Kentucky, what people come to mind? Pioneers like Daniel Boone, politicians like Abraham Lincoln, athletes like Muhammad Ali, musicians like Loretta Lynn and movie stars like George Clooney. But can you name any famous scientists from Kentucky? Probably not. Yet Kentucky has a rich scientific heritage that every citizen of the state can be proud of. In fact, four scientists born and raised in Kentucky have won a Nobel Prize.

The sad fact is that science doesn't always get the credit it deserves. What accounts for this state of affairs? For one thing, science is neither a spectator sport nor a performing art. Thus, science is not as readily accessible to the average person. Whereas anyone can appreciate an outstanding athletic or musical performance, not everyone can understand and appreciate an important scientific discovery. Science is done behind the scenes and is usually done by teams of people. This makes it more difficult to award credit to a single individual. Finally, journalists writing and reporting the news often have little or no training in science and may be uncomfortable trying to explain complicated ideas to their watchers and readers.

Also, there is a problem in this country that seems particularly acute in Kentucky. A significant fraction of the population just doesn't trust science or scientists. They look askance at egg-headed intellectuals and know-it-all experts. Even some of Kentucky's past and present political leaders address problems by going with their gut rather than following the data. Facts, reason and rationality be damned! And many in the state reject well-established scientific principles such as the theory of evolution. After all, Kentucky has its very own Creation Museum. This anti-scientific attitude can be dangerous. This is evidenced by the fact that many people in Kentucky stubbornly refused to get a COVID vaccine, putting their lives at risk because of their political philosophy.

This book is a small step toward solving this big problem. It gives science the credit it deserves by celebrating Kentucky's scientists and their accomplishments. For this book, I am using a rather expansive definition of science to include physicians, inventors and science educators. Two criteria guided my selection

The Nobel Prize Medal. The prize is awarded each year in chemistry, physics, medicine or physiology, literature, economics and peace. *Shutterstock.*

of the seventeen individuals. First, their contributions to science, invention or science education had to be scientifically or historically significant. Second, a large fraction of their lives had to be spent in Kentucky. In fact, most of the scientists were born and raised in the state. Practical considerations also played a role in the selection. For example, adequate and accessible biographical information had to be available about the person.

There were a few outstanding individuals who were left out of the book but deserve at least a mention. Harry Yandell Benedict, born and raised in Louisville, was an astronomer and mathematician who became president of the University of Texas. Paul Ewald, a professor at the University of Louisville, is an expert in the emerging field of evolutionary medicine. G. Scott Hubbard, born in Lexington and raised in Elizabethtown, was a NASA scientist and administrator. And Isaac Chuang, born in Corbin, is a pioneer in the field of quantum computing.

The book begins with a brief history of science in Kentucky, along with a short explanation of how modern scientists do their work. The rest of the book presents biographical sketches of scientists, inventors and science educators from the Bluegrass State. The biographies are presented in chronological order according to birth year. Each biographical sketch begins with the person's field, their major contribution, their connection to the state and a quote. The biographies include a simple explanation of their discoveries.

I hope this book will inform the general public about Kentucky's rich scientific heritage and inspire future generations to consider a scientific career. Let us begin!

SCIENCE IN KENTUCKY, THEN AND NOW

S cience in the Bluegrass State began when physicians made their way across the Appalachians into Kentucky Territory to treat sick and injured settlers. One of those early doctors was Ephraim McDowell, whose family settled in Danville around 1784, when he was thirteen. Kentucky would not be granted statehood until 1792. McDowell, who is the first scientist portrayed in this book, would perform the world's first successful surgical removal of an ovarian tumor.

The story of science in Kentucky is closely linked to the history of its institutions of higher learning. The first college in Kentucky (and the first west of the Allegheny Mountains) was Transylvania University, established in 1780 by an act of the Virginia Assembly with the support of then governor Thomas Jefferson. The school began as a religious seminary in a log cabin near Danville, where the first classes were held in 1785. In 1789, the school moved to Lexington, and by 1799, it had become known as Transylvania University. Law and medical schools were also established, and by the 1820s, the school ranked among the best in the entire country. In 1820, Professor Samuel Brown founded the first medical fraternity of its kind, Kappa Lambda of Hippocrates. Branches of the fraternity eventually led to the founding of the American Medical Association. Until the Civil War, Transylvania University was the dominate academic institution in Kentucky. Ambitious students from all over the South flocked to its halls of learning.

The Civil War interrupted instruction at Transylvania, with some buildings turned into makeshift hospitals for Union troops. After the war,

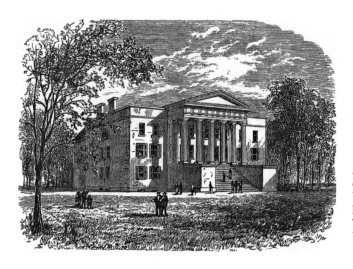

An 1879 drawing of Kentucky University, later known as Transylvania University. *Wikimedia Commons.*

Transylvania merged with Bacon College in Harrodsburg to form Kentucky University, a name the institution used for the next forty-three years. In 1878, Kentucky University's Agricultural and Mechanical College became the state's new land grant university: the University of Kentucky. In 1908, Kentucky University was again renamed Transylvania University to avoid confusion with the University of Kentucky.

In its early days, Transylvania had several notable science faculty members who were presumably some of the first scientists in the state. Among them was Daniel Drake, a faculty member from 1817 to 1818 and dean from 1825 until 1827. Drake taught medicine and made contributions in botany, geology and meteorology. In 1827, Drake founded the *Western Journal of the Medical and Physical Sciences* and was its editor until 1848. Drake is a significant figure in the history of medical science in the United States. Constantine Samuel Rafinesque was a professor of botany from 1819 until 1826. Rafinesque was a self-taught naturalist who collected plants and animals from around the state and named thousands of species. Charles Caldwell was a professor of medicine from 1819 until 1837 and helped turn the medical school into one of the best in the country. He convinced the Kentucky General Assembly to purchase $10,000 worth of science and medical books from France, some of which are still held in the university library. Unfortunately, Caldwell could be difficult and abrasive, traits that eventually led to his dismissal.

Today, Transylvania University is a small school of about one thousand students and sits in the shadow of its much larger neighbor, the University of Kentucky. But no school in Kentucky, and few schools elsewhere, can

An aerial view of Transylvania University in Lexington. It was founded in 1780 and was the first university in Kentucky. *Wikimedia Commons.*

match the illustrious list of Transylvania alumni. That list includes 2 vice-presidents, 2 Supreme Court justices, 34 ambassadors, 36 governors, 50 U.S. senators and 101 U.S. representatives.

In modern times, most scientific research in Kentucky takes place at one of the state's two flagship research universities: the University of Louisville (UL) and the University of Kentucky (UK). Scientific research is also done at smaller colleges and universities and by government agencies and private industries. The older of the two institutions, the University of Louisville, was established in 1798 and was the first city-owned public university in the country. The University of Louisville School of Medicine is the ninth-oldest medical school in the United States and has an impressive list of accolades. It was the first to offer the services of a civilian ambulance, the first to offer an accident service (known today as an emergency department) and one of the first to house a blood bank. Teams of doctors at the UL medical school performed the first five successful hand transplants in the United States starting in 1999 and the first self-contained artificial heart transplant in 2001.

Founded in 1798, the University of Louisville is one of Kentucky's two research universities. It was the first city-owned public university in the nation. *Wikimedia Commons*.

An aerial view of the campus of the University of Kentucky. Founded in 1865, it is one of the state's two research universities. *Shutterstock*.

The state's largest university is the University of Kentucky, with over thirty thousand students. As previously mentioned, it was founded in 1865 as Kentucky University's Agricultural and Mechanical College and became the University of Kentucky in 1878. Today, UK offers majors in nearly every scientific field. UK's College of Pharmacy ranks sixth in the nation, and its programs in agriculture, plant sciences and entomology are also highly ranked. According to the National Science Foundation, in 2018, UK spent $393 million on research and development activities, whereas UL spent $176 million.

There is one other place that has played a major role in the scientific history of Kentucky: the Paducah Gaseous Diffusion Plant. From 1952 until 2013, the plant, owned by the U.S. Department of Energy, produced enriched uranium. During the 1950s, the uranium was used for nuclear weapons. From the 1960s onward, it was used for fuel in commercial nuclear power plants. And for a while, Paducah promoted itself as the "Atomic City."

What is enriched uranium? When uranium ore is dug out of the ground, most of it is a form (the technical term is isotope) of uranium that won't split or fission. The fissioning of uranium is how the energy is released. Only a tiny percentage of natural uranium is the form that can be used in nuclear weapons or in nuclear power. The useful, fissionable form of uranium has to be separated from the rest of the uranium. This is a difficult task to accomplish because it's all uranium, so chemically speaking, it all behaves the same way. The difference between the forms of uranium is a small variance in the mass. So, to separate the forms of uranium, one has to take advantage of this difference in mass. It is the uranium atoms with the lighter mass that undergo fission.

One way of separating the forms of uranium is gaseous diffusion. In gaseous diffusion, the uranium atoms are combined with six fluorine atoms to form molecules of uranium hexafluoride (UF_6) gas. Most of the gas molecules have the nonfissionable form of uranium, but a few have the fissile form. The gas is then forced through a semipermeable membrane. The lighter molecules with the fissile uranium will pass (diffuse) more easily through the membrane than the heavier molecules. This accomplishes the separation, but only to a tiny degree. To get enough separation, the process must be repeated thousands of times. The diffusion chambers were contained within giant cylinders called converters. This is what the Paducah plant did until 2013.

Workers standing in front of a converter at the Paducah Gaseous Diffusion Plant. *Shutterstock.*

An aerial view of the 750-acre Paducah Gaseous Diffusion Plant as it appeared in 1964. *Wikimedia Commons.*

A massive effort is now underway to clean up the site. Tons of depleted uranium left over from the processing is just sitting at the site. But the waste material may be useful. Billionaire Bill Gates has invested in a nuclear power company called TerraPower, which claims the waste material could be converted into useful fuel that could power the entire country for hundreds of years. The ultimate fate of the waste material is yet to be determined.

2

HOW SCIENCE WORKS

Now that we know where most scientists work, the next question is this: How do scientists do their work? How do scientists do scientific research? Back in elementary school, everybody learned about the scientific method; the steps are usually presented as follows. First, a scientist has to formulate a problem, a question about the natural world. Then they make a hypothesis, a guess about the answer to the problem. It should be emphasized that the hypothesis is an educated guess—using all their knowledge and training, what does the scientist think the answer is? A hypothesis is not a random guess—a scientist doesn't just write the possible answers on little slips of paper, put them all in a hat, shake the hat and draw one. The next step is the heart and soul of science: a scientist tests the hypothesis by doing an experiment or by making observations. In other words, a scientist tests their ideas against reality. Experiments usually involve taking measurements and collecting data. Finally, a scientist analyzes their data to see if it supports their hypothesis or not.

To give a simple example of the scientific method, consider the following question: How do stars shine? In other words, what is the energy source of the stars? A hypothesis might be "a star shines because it is a big lump of burning coal in outer space." Next, an experiment is done. One might burn samples of coal under carefully controlled conditions and measure how much energy is released. Finally, one could compare the energy released by coal to the energy released by a star like the Sun. If the energy released by the coal is comparable to the energy released by the Sun, then the

A scientist at work in her lab. Usually, scientists work in small teams. *Shutterstock.*

hypothesis is confirmed. If, on the other hand, the energy released by coal is not comparable to the energy released by the Sun, then the hypothesis is wrong. (For the record, this problem has already been researched. We now know that stars aren't lumps of burning coal. Instead, they are giant spheres of hydrogen plasma undergoing a process called nuclear fusion, which transforms the hydrogen into helium and, in the process, releases energy.)

Though this presents the steps of the scientific method as a simple, straightforward, cookbook-style recipe for doing science, please understand that science isn't always so neat and tidy. For example, luck has played an important role in many scientific discoveries. A petri dish accidentally left open led Alexander Fleming to the discovery of penicillin, and a rock left sitting on a photographic plate led Henri Becquerel to the discovery of radioactivity. Also, the steps aren't always followed in the order presented. Sometimes experiments are done to generate hypotheses. Finally, it isn't always the same scientist or group of scientists who do all the steps. In physics, theoreticians come up with hypotheses—guesses about how the universe works. They then hand off the scientific baton to experimentalists who test the hypotheses. The point is that science is much more complicated than the step-by-step process we all learned back in elementary school.

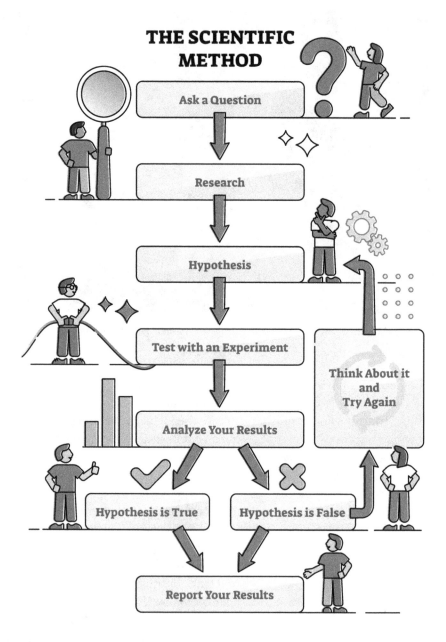

A diagram showing the usual steps of the scientific method. But be aware that science is not always as simple and straightforward. *Shutterstock.*

Once scientists have completed their research, how do they communicate the results to the scientific community? The main way a scientist communicates is by writing a paper and submitting it for publication in a scientific journal. When the editor of the journal receives the paper, they will send it to one or several experts in that particular area of science. Those experts will then read and critique the paper, checking for clarity and looking for mistakes. Some of the questions the reviewer might ask are: Is the conclusion supported by the data? Are the steps of the procedure clearly outlined? This critically important process is called peer review, the experts who critique the paper are called referees and journals that use the process are called refereed journals. This is all done anonymously; the author does not know who the referees are. The referees will then make a recommendation to the editor as to whether the paper should be accepted for publication. There are three possible recommendations: the paper can be accepted for publication, it can be accepted with revisions or it can be rejected. If it is rejected, the authors are free to submit it to another publication. Sometimes, scientists have a pecking order of publications they plan to submit to, starting with the most prestigious journal. If the paper is rejected, they move to the next, slightly less prestigious journal. The process of peer review can be thought of as scientific quality control—it's in place to ensure that the papers the journal choses to publish meet the highest standards expected in science.

There are hundreds of scientific journals. The two most prestigious journals in the world are *Science*, published by the American Association for the Advancement of Science, and *Nature*, published in London. Both are published weekly, and, unlike most journals, which focus on a specific field, *Science* and *Nature* span the entire range of scientific disciplines. Most journals focus on a specific scientific field like astronomy, biology, chemistry and physics. And there are journals that home in on a tiny subfield of science. But beware, there are also hundreds of fake scientific journals. These journals have no peer review process; they will publish any paper as long as the authors pay a fee. Thus, when surveying the scientific literature for reliable information, it is important to make sure that the source is a peer-reviewed journal (sometimes called a refereed journal).

Despite this rigorous procedure of peer review, sometimes mistakes are made. One famous example is the supposed connection between vaccines and autism. In 1998, Andrew Wakefield, a British physician, published a paper in the prestigious British medical journal *The Lancet*. The paper made the fraudulent claim that the measles, mumps and rubella vaccine was linked to autism. The fraud was exposed by a newspaper investigation. In 2010, the paper was retracted, but the damage had been done. Many people still believe that vaccines cause autism. The scientific consensus is that there is no causal connection between any vaccine and autism.

A final question one might ask about science is: Who pays for all this? Funding for science in the United States comes from a variety of sources, including wealthy individuals and private industries. But the main source of funding comes from various agencies of the federal government. Two of the agencies that provide the bulk of funding for basic scientific research are the National Science Foundation (NSF) and the National Institutes of Health (NIH). With a budget of over $8 billion in 2020, the NSF accounts for about a quarter of the total science funding to academic institutions. The NIH funds research in medical fields. With a budget of over $40 billion in 2020, the NIH provides about 28 percent of funding for medical research in the country. Other federal agencies also have funds available to support research. These agencies include the Department of Energy (DOE), the Environmental Protection Agency (EPA), the Centers for Disease Control (CDC), the National Oceanic and Atmospheric Administration (NOAA) and National Aeronautics and Space Administration (NASA). Federal funding for scientific research and development fluctuates with the political winds but is usually between 2 and 3 percent of the total federal budget. Of course, the money from these agencies ultimately comes from taxpayers. So, between two and three cents out of every federal tax dollar goes to support scientific research in the United States.

Partially as a result of this federal investment, the United States currently leads the world in most areas of science. This wasn't always the case. During the 1700s and most of the 1800s, our young country lagged behind Europe. After all, we had other things to do: explore and settle vast new regions, grow enough food to feed everybody and fight the bloody Civil War. That began to change in the late 1880s, as American inventors like Thomas Edison, Nikola Tesla and Alexander Graham Bell developed new devices that improved daily life. And things really changed as a result of World War II. An influx of brilliant immigrant scientists from central Europe came to the United States and elevated our science. Many of them participated in the Manhattan Project, the successful effort to build an atomic bomb. The massive project demonstrated the value of cooperation between scientists and the government. After World War II, Europe, Russia and Japan were devastated, and China fell under oppressive communist rule. The United States had little competition and became dominant in science. One indicator of this transition is the number of scientific Nobel

Prizes awarded to various countries. Before World War II, European countries such as Germany and the United Kingdom were awarded the most Nobel Prizes. After the war, U.S. scientists won the bulk of the prizes.

This scientific balance of power is beginning to shift. The countries of the European Union and Southeast Asia are quickly catching up to the United States. China, for example, is making massive investments in research and development. This is not a bad thing—it's good for humanity. Science is not a zero-sum game. But in order to keep up, the United States must continue to invest heavily in science.

Science isn't perfect because the human beings who do science aren't perfect. But it's the best tool we've got. Instead of making stuff up, science figures things out. It was science that came up with a vaccine for COVID, and it will be science that solves the problem of climate change. (For an excellent discussion of the problems science faces, see Stuart Ritchie's book *Science Fictions*.)

Now come with me as we celebrate science by learning about the lives of seventeen scientific heroes from the Bluegrass State.

3

EPHRAIM McDOWELL

1771–1830

Field | Medicine
Major Contribution | In 1809, McDowell surgically removed an ovarian tumor from a patient. It was the first time such a procedure had been successfully performed.
Kentucky Connection | Lived in Kentucky from age thirteen

> *All honor, then we say, to the man who thus paved the way to a new path of humanity, since so nobly trodden by his successors. All honor to the man who had the nerve and the skill to do that which no man had ever dared to do before! All honor to the heroic woman, who with death literally staring her in the face, was the first to submit calmly and resignedly what certainly was, at the time, a surgical experiment.*
>
> *—Dr. Samuel Gross, professor of surgery at the University of Louisville, in an 1879 speech honoring McDowell*

EPHRAIM McDOWELL was born in Rockbridge County in central Virginia on November 11, 1771. He was the ninth of eleven children born to Samuel McDowell and Mary McClung McDowell. We know little about McDowell's childhood and adolescence. He probably attended school at the Liberty Hall Academy in Rockbridge County since his father was a trustee.

A portrait of Ephraim McDowell. *Shutterstock.*

When McDowell was thirteen, the family moved to Danville, Kentucky, where he attended a nearby seminary. Much of what we know about young Ephraim comes to us through his granddaughter Mary Y. Ridenbaugh, who wrote a biography of McDowell in 1890 based on interviews with family members. According to Ridenbaugh, McDowell was curious, thoughtful and studious, someone who preferred reading books over playing games. His father was a member of a political club, and as a result, there were probably many stimulating family conversations and debates.

As a teenager, McDowell was a handsome young man standing nearly six feet tall with dark hair and eyes. He was witty, enjoyed conversation and had an engaging personality. McDowell typically dressed in black with silk stockings and ruffled linen and did not indulge in alcohol or tobacco, although later in his life he would occasionally have a few sips of whiskey. He always presented a tidy appearance, a personal habit that he would apply in his future career.

At age nineteen, McDowell became a doctor. At that time in America, prospective physicians didn't just pack their bags for medical school. (In fact, there was, at the time, only one medical school in America, founded in 1765 at the College of Philadelphia, now the University of Pennsylvania.) Instead, one became an apprentice to a practicing physician for two or three years. The apprentice swept floors, built fires and did other chores around the office, in addition to paying the physician a stipend. In return, the apprentice accompanied the doctor on visits to patients, discussed the cases and treatments and had access to the doctor's collection of medical textbooks. If the apprentice completed the tasks to the satisfaction of his mentor, he was named a doctor of medicine and presented with a certificate. And that was the end of his medical training.

Of course, the practice of medicine in those days bore little resemblance to modern medical science. Most physicians used a single theory to explain all diseases. For example, the famous Scottish physician William Cullen believed all diseases were caused by a disturbed nervous system created by excitement or irritation. His treatment was to calm the patient through a combination of bloodletting, sweating and induced vomiting. An apprentice was trained only in the method espoused by their mentoring physician.

In 1791, McDowell journeyed back over the Appalachian Mountains to apprentice under Dr. Alexander Humphreys of Staunton, Virginia. Humphreys was a well-known and distinguished doctor who was educated at the University of Edinburgh in Scotland, which was considered the best medical school in the world. Humphreys insisted his students learn anatomy by dissecting human bodies. Public opinion at the time opposed the medical use of human cadavers; desperate men would rob fresh graves and sell the bodies. Humphreys probably got some of his cadavers from grave robbers.

After completing his apprenticeship, McDowell continued his medical education at Edinburgh, no doubt influenced by Humphreys. After a six-month journey, McDowell arrived in Edinburgh during the 1792–93 academic year, although the exact date is unknown. He attended lectures and borrowed books from the library, including a book called *Female Complaints* by Hamilton, a title that showed he had an interest in the subject. During his second year at the university, McDowell took a private course from Dr. John Bell, a celebrated surgeon and popular lecturer. In particular, Bell taught McDowell about diseases of the ovaries, admitting that such afflictions were hopeless and that surgical removal of the organ was a procedure that had never been undertaken successfully.

Whether McDowell actually graduated with a medical degree from Edinburgh is unclear. McDowell's name does not appear on the university's list of graduates, and no diploma has ever been found. And yet McDowell later signed his two published medical papers as "Ephraim McDowell, M.D.," and it seems unlikely that McDowell, who always insisted on accuracy, would have added the "M.D." unless he had earned the title. Some historians think the designation was an honorary degree given to McDowell later in his life.

In 1795, McDowell arrived back in Danville, and word quickly spread that he had attended the University of Edinburgh, the most prestigious medical school in the world. As a result, his practice began to flourish, and patients came to him from hundreds of miles away. He treated wounds, set fractures, performed amputations and repaired hernias. At least one account claims he was the first surgeon in the country to perform a Caesarean section; however, this story cannot been confirmed because no report was ever made.

McDowell was especially adept at removing bladder stones. In 1812, a seventeen-year-old Tennessee boy named James K. Polk came to see McDowell in Danville. He was chronically ill from a urinary tract infection and suffered from intense bladder pain. McDowell diagnosed the problem as a bladder stone and removed it. Polk returned home with the stone in his pocket and later became the eleventh president of the United States. Polk had no children, so it is possible that the procedure left him impotent.

In 1802, McDowell married Sarah Shelby, the eighteen-year-old daughter of Kentucky's first governor, Isaac Shelby. She was described as beautiful, reserved and charming. The couple had eight children—two boys and six girls—although only five survived to adulthood. McDowell bought some land outside of Danville, where he established a farm and built a large house with a wide porch and a peaceful view across a lake. He named the house Cambuskenneth after a village in Scotland, near Edinburgh. (The original house burned down around 1900, but a house with a similar design was built in its place and remains there today.) The family lived on the farm in the summer and also maintained a house in Danville where they lived during the winter. McDowell hired an overseer to run the farm since his medical practice took all his time. Like many wealthy southern landowners of the time, McDowell owned several slaves.

McDowell accumulated an excellent medical library and, in his leisure time, enjoyed reading history and poetry, especially the works of Scottish poet Robert Burns. Occasionally, he recited Burns's works with a Scottish accent that he had picked up in Edinburgh. McDowell enjoyed reading, but he did not enjoy writing. Unfortunately for medical science, he wrote only two short professional reports. His lack of writing skills hindered him from sharing his considerable medical knowledge with his colleagues.

Over time, McDowell established a reputation as a brave and resourceful surgeon with nerves of steel. He insisted his patients understand the risks of surgery before agreeing to undertake the procedure and made sure that his assistants were clear about their duties. McDowell was devoutly religious and prayed before every operation.

In 1809, McDowell, who had practiced medicine for fourteen years, performed the operation that would make him famous. The procedure involved removing a tumor from a woman's ovaries (ovariotomy), an operation that had never successfully been done before anywhere in the world. At the time, physicians thought it was virtually impossible to survive abdominal surgery. Why? Because a membrane called the peritoneum encloses the abdominal organs, including the stomach and intestines. Physicians insisted that cutting open the peritoneum could cause fatal inflammation. Even if the inflammation was avoided, the surgeon risked puncturing the intestines and releasing fecal matter into the body cavity, resulting in a fatal infection. Even today, abdominal surgery is riskier than many other types of surgery for the same reason.

He performed the famous surgery on a patient named Jane Todd Crawford who lived in Greene County, Kentucky, about sixty miles southwest of Danville. It was December, but McDowell made the arduous trip on horseback to meet the patient. He had been summoned by two physicians who thought that Crawford, although she was forty-six, was pregnant with twins but past term. Upon arriving, McDowell immediately examined Crawford, a small woman whose abdomen, according to McDowell, "had become so pendulous as to reach almost to her knees." He later recalled the encounter in a letter to a medical student:

> *Upon examination per vaginam I soon ascertained that she was not pregnant; but had a large tumor in the abdomen which moved easily from side to side. I told the lady that I could do her no good and candidly stated to her, her deplorable situation; informed her that John Bell, Hunter, Hay, and A. Wood, four of the first and most eminent surgeons in England and Scotland, had uniformly declared in their lectures that such was the danger of peritoneal inflammation, that opening the abdomen to extract the tumor was inevitable death. But notwithstanding this, if she thought herself prepared to die, I would take the lump from her if she could come to Danville.*

McDowell's clear, thorough and honest communication to his patient about her condition is an early example of what is now known as informed consent. His insistence that she come to Danville was to ensure that he could attend to her recovery. Despite the risks, Crawford agreed to the surgery and made the hard winter journey to Danville on horseback. According to McDowell's granddaughter, he wanted to perform the surgery on a Sunday morning so that the prayers of churchgoers would be with him. However, according to a letter written by McDowell, the operation was done on Christmas Day, which, in 1809, was on a Monday.

As the procedure began, Jane Crawford lay down on her back on a table and removed any clothing that might be in the way. McDowell did the operation without anesthesia; ether was not used for that purpose until 1846. He did it with no knowledge of the germ theory of disease; Louis Pasteur's discoveries weren't made until the 1860s. And he did it without antiseptics; Joseph Lister would not develop his ideas about a sterile environment until 1865.

As soon as McDowell made the first nine-inch incision, the massive tumor pushed Crawford's intestines out onto the table. Keep in mind that poor Jane Crawford was fully conscious throughout the entire procedure. Her pain must have been unimaginable, but she had no choice. Mercifully, it took McDowell only twenty-five minutes to complete the operation and remove the twenty-two-pound tumor. Speed was important in surgical procedures to minimize blood loss, reduce shock and limit the risk of infection. Crawford survived the operation. She was up and moving after five days and, after recuperating for twenty-five days, got back on her horse and rode home. She lived another thirty-two years. McDowell had not only proved that removing an ovarian tumor was possible but also showed that surgery on the abdominal region was survivable. For this accomplishment, McDowell has been called "the father of ovariotomy" and one of the founding fathers of abdominal surgery.

What factors account for McDowell's successful surgery? First, he was an expert at anatomy and carefully planned his surgery before cutting anyone open. Big tumors often have enlarged blood vessels that could cause problematic bleeding. McDowell knew exactly where he would have to bind blood vessels to stop the bleeding. Second, he removed as much blood and other secretions as possible by turning the patient on her side at the end of the surgery. This allowed the fluids to drain out of the body and prevented potential complications. Third, McDowell's method of suturing allowed any remaining fluids to drain out of the body. Finally, McDowell was scrupulous about keeping the environment clean during the procedure. This included bathing the intestines in warm water.

In 1813, McDowell performed a second ovariotomy on an enslaved woman. To lessen the pain and avoid surgery, he gave her mercury for three or four months. Mercury was commonly used in the 1800s as a treatment for pain, constipation and depression before its toxicity was understood. When the woman still couldn't perform her duties, McDowell agreed to do the surgery. This time, he gave the woman cherry bounce to lessen the shock. (Cherry bounce was a popular alcoholic drink in the 1800s that involving soaking cherries in whiskey or some other alcoholic beverage.) Once again, McDowell was sure his patient would not survive, and once again, she did. McDowell performed a third ovariotomy in May 1816, again on an enslaved woman. She recovered in two weeks and resumed her work as a cook for a large family.

In 1817, after three successful ovariotomies, McDowell published a report on the procedure in the *Eclectic Repertory and Analytical Review*, a medical journal based in Philadelphia. News of the surgery eventually made its way into European medical journals, and by 1824, the successful procedure was well known throughout the medical establishment.

Above: The McDowell house in Danville, Kentucky. McDowell performed the first ovariotomy here in 1809. The house is now a museum. *Christopher L. Riley/Wikimedia Commons.*

Left: A statue of Ephraim McDowell rests in the U.S. Capitol building in Washington, D.C. A copy sits in the Kentucky State Capitol in Frankfort. *Architect of the Capitol/Wikimedia Commons.*

McDowell continued to perform ovariotomies. Nine surgeries were reported, of which only two resulted in the patient's death. McDowell's nephew Dr. William M. McDowell later stated that Ephraim completed eighteen ovariotomies. Most notable among the subsequent operations was the sixth, done in 1822 at the Nashville, Tennessee home of Andrew Jackson, who became the seventh president of the United States. Jackson helped comfort the patient during the operation, in which the tumor was not actually removed but simply drained of fluid.

Ephraim McDowell died on June 20, 1830, at age fifty-nine. He suffered from severe stomach pains, nausea and vomiting brought on, so he thought, by eating berries with poisonous insects or eggs. It is now suspected that McDowell likely died from a ruptured appendix. His grave is in McDowell Park in Danville.

McDowell is remembered in several ways. His home in Danville is now a museum that has been designated as a National Historic Landmark and is open to the public. It is not clear which room of the house was used as an operating room. The esteem in which the State of Kentucky holds McDowell is evidenced by his statue being found in Statuary Hall in the U.S. Capitol in Washington, D.C. On the right of the statue sits a bowl holding the ovarian tumor. The other of the two statues representing Kentucky is that of Henry Clay. It is likely that the two men knew each other because Clay defended McDowell's brother-in-law in a legal matter. A model of the statue resides in the state capitol in Frankfort. There is also a granite monument to McDowell in Danville dedicated in 1879 by the Kentucky Medical Association. On December 30, 1959, the U.S. Postal Service issued a four-cent commemorative stamp on the 150th anniversary of McDowell's famous operation. Ephraim McDowell Regional Medical Center in Danville is named in his honor.

McDowell's brave patient, Jane Todd Crawford, died on March 30, 1842, at age seventy-eight. We can find her grave in the Johnson Cemetery on Indiana State Road #36, a mile and a half north of Graysville, Indiana. There is also a large monument to Crawford in McDowell Park in Danville.

4

JAMES ESPY

1785–1860

Field | Meteorology
Major Contribution | Espy correctly explained how clouds form.
Kentucky Connection | Espy spent part of his childhood in Kentucky
and graduated from Transylvania University.

*I leave all this to the future, sure that its adaptation to the
uses of life must one day be seen and acknowledged.*
—Espy, quoted by his niece Mrs. L.M. Morehead

JAMES POLLARD ESPY was born near Pittsburgh, Pennsylvania, on May 9, 1785. He was the youngest of ten children. When he was an infant, the family moved to the Bluegrass region of Kentucky. After several years, the family's opposition to slavery prompted another move to the Miami Valley in Ohio. At age eighteen, Espy returned to Kentucky as a student at Transylvania University in Lexington. While at Transylvania, an older brother visited James and reported: "I found him at the university, where he had made considerable progress in the dead languages and in general science. He shows an ardent desire for knowledge, and promises to be both intelligent and useful."

Upon graduating in 1808, Espy moved to Xenia, Ohio, where he studied and practiced law for four years. But he enjoyed teaching more than lawyering. According to a niece, "His love for teaching amounted to enthusiasm, and, although he completed his law studies, he finally abandoned the idea of choosing the law as his profession, and determined to follow the bent of his inclination, and become a conscientious instructor of youth." She added, "He considered this a noble profession, and even in old age was fond of drawing out young students to talk over their lessons with him, both hearing them and asking them questions."

After his time in Ohio (or possibly before—sources differ regarding the timeline), he taught at an academy in Cumberland, Maryland. In 1812, he married his sixteen-year-old cousin Margaret Pollard and took her last name as his middle name. Margaret supported her husband's teaching and scientific work. A colleague said, "There was one person who had more influence upon him than all others besides, stimulating him to progress, and urging him forward in each step with a zeal which never flagged—this was his wife."

In 1817, Espy became a teacher at the Franklin Institute in Philadelphia. According to A.D. Bache, a fellow professor, Espy developed into "one of the best classical and mathematical instructors in Philadelphia." During this time, Espy read some papers on meteorology by English scientists John Dalton and John Daniell and became interested in the subject. Around the year 1828, Espy began his own investigations into meteorological phenomena. He was especially interested in storms.

Most of Espy's weather research was done outdoors. A friend who visited Espy's Philadelphia home described his laboratory: "The high fence enclosing the small yard was of smooth plank, painted white, while the space enclosed was filled with vessels of water and numerous thermometers for determining the dew-point. The white fence, when last seen by the narrator, was so covered with figures and calculations that not a spot remained for another sum or column."

To aid him in his research, Espy invented an instrument called a "nephelescope" (cloud watcher). The device, consisting of an air pump, a vessel and a barometer, allowed Espy to measure the drop in temperature of a gas when the pressure decreased. It was a predecessor of modern cloud chambers and was one of the first instruments used to study cloud physics. Espy also flew kites to collect data on the direction of winds and the height of clouds.

In 1834, Espy became meteorologist for both the Franklin Institute and the American Philosophical Society of Philadelphia. He convinced the Pennsylvania legislature to budget $4,000 to equip an observer in every county with a barometer, a thermometer and a rain gauge. The observers would collect data and send it to Espy. This resulted in the first meteorological reports in the records of Congress.

By 1836, Espy had given up teaching so that he could devote all of his time and energy to the study of weather. He lived off his savings and the money he earned by lecturing to popular audiences. Because of these talks, Espy became known as the "Storm King."

In September 1840, Espy traveled to Europe, where he gave a lecture on his theory of storms to the British Science Association. Later that year, he made a presentation to the French Academy of Science. In the discussion that followed the talk, one of the French professors proclaimed, "France has its Cuvier, England its Newton, America its Espy." Upon his return to America in 1841, Espy published his most important work, *The Philosophy of Storms*.

Unfortunately for Espy, his theory about storms turned out to be incorrect. And he put forth a few other kooky ideas. For example, Espy had noticed that smoke from Indian bonfires and factory chimneys seemed to attract rain clouds. Based on this casual and unscientific observation, Espy concluded that smoke causes rain. He therefore proposed a scheme to regulate rainfall. Anytime rain was needed, he suggested starting forest fires in the Appalachian Mountains. The resulting smoke would blow over the eastern United States and create a deluge.

But Espy's ideas about how clouds form were largely correct. According to Espy, clouds form when masses of less dense warm air rise into the cooler upper atmosphere. There, water vapor condenses into tiny droplets. The atmosphere exerts an upward buoyant force on the droplets that keep them suspended in the air. And voilà: a cloud is born.

Espy's emphasis on water vapor foreshadowed the idea that the gas plays a key role in weather changes. To understand why, we first need to know that air is a mixture of gases. The main constituents are nitrogen (78 percent), oxygen (21 percent), argon (0.93 percent) and trace amounts of other gases, including carbon dioxide and water vapor. The concentration of these gases is fixed except for water vapor, which can vary widely depending on local conditions. In deserts, the concentration is almost zero; in rain forests, it can be a few percent.

Also, water vapor is the only atmospheric gas that changes back and forth between a gas and a liquid in the range of temperatures normally found on Earth. As water changes from a gas into a liquid (condensation), heat is released. When water changes from a liquid to a gas (evaporation), heat is absorbed. Thus, as it changes state, water can dump heat into or suck heat out of the surrounding air. This process leads to changes in temperature and pressure. Zones of air with higher or lower pressure are called fronts. The fronts collide, creating changes in the weather.

In 1843, Espy was chosen as the first meteorologist to work for the federal government. He moved to Washington, D.C., where he was employed first by the military. Then, in 1848, he was assigned to the Smithsonian Institution. During his Washington years, he worked with newspapers and telegraph companies to establish daily weather bulletins from around the country.

Espy ended his work in Washington, D.C., in 1859 and spent the next few months visiting relatives. While visiting his nephew in Cincinnati, Espy had a stroke and died on January 17, 1860, at age seventy-four. A colleague remembers him personally as "eminently social, full of bonhomie and enthusiasm, easily kindling into a glow by social mental action." Espy is buried in the cemetery at Harrisburg, Pennsylvania, next to his wife, who preceded him in death by ten years.

Professor J.E. McDonald at the University of Arizona's Institute for Atmospheric Physics assessed Espy's scientific contributions as follows:

Although he cannot be counted one of the most eminent of early meteorologists, he made contributions of lasting value. Working at a time when it was necessary to break through tangled thickets of ignorance and error to come upon even simple scientific truths, Espy is to be remembered as one of the pioneers of nineteenth-century meteorology and of cloud thermodynamics, in particular.

NATHAN STUBBLEFIELD

1860–1928

Field | Invention
Major Contribution | Invented a wireless telephone system
Kentucky Connection | Born and lived in or near Murray his entire life

> *Nathan Stubblefield Raises Vegetables for Market in Order That He May Live, But Has for Ten Years Devoted All of His Spare Time to Electrical Experiments, Until Now He Has Perfected a Wireless Telephone System Over Which Messages Are Distinctly Heard at a Mile.*
>
> —St. Louis Post-Dispatch, *January 12, 1902*

NATHAN BEVERLY STUBBLEFIELD was born on November 22, 1860, in Murray, in far western Kentucky. He was the third of four sons born to William Stubblefield and Victoria Bowman. William, a Confederate captain during the Civil War, was an attorney known around town as "Captain Billie." His successful law practice meant that the family was well off financially and could afford to employ a governess who tutored young Nathan.

When he was older, Stubblefield attended a boarding school in nearby Farmington with the rather odd name, at least to modern ears, of the "Male and Female Institute." At the time, there were no high schools in the area, and the institute provided the best education available. Stubblefield's mother died of scarlet fever in 1869, and a few years later, his father remarried the governess, Clara Janes. Then in 1874, his father contracted pneumonia and died, leaving Stubblefield in the care of his stepmother and former governess.

His father's death brought an end to Stubblefield's formal education, but his hungry mind found fresh nourishment from the periodicals available in the offices of the local newspaper, the *Calloway County Times*. Initially, Stubblefield was drawn to the pages of a magazine called *Practical Farmer*, but soon, another periodical, *Scientific American*, captured his attention. The two magazines reflected the endeavors that would occupy Nathan for the rest of his life: farming and science.

In 1881, Stubblefield married seventeen-year-old Ada Mae Buchannan, a Paducah girl he had known at the institute. The couple moved in to a little two-room house that sat on an acre of his father's land. Stubblefield farmed the land and grew enough fruits and vegetables to feed themselves with enough left over to sell in Murray on Saturdays. To help promote his produce, Stubblefield always wore his best suit and hat to market. The couple had nine children: Carrie (1885), Barnard Bowman (1887), Frederic (1888), Patti Lee (1890), Victoria Edison (1892), Nathan Franklin (1895), Oliver Jefferson (1897), Helen Gould (1901) and William Tesla (1903). At the time, the infant mortality rate was high, and three of the children—Carrie, Frederic and William Tesla—died at young ages. The children's names reflected Stubblefield's interest in electricity, with Victoria Edison, Nathan Franklin and William Tesla all named after famous scientists and inventors in the field.

With more mouths to feed, Stubblefield expanded his farm onto his late father's land. But the income from the little farm wasn't enough to support a big family, so Stubblefield decided to try to transform his interest in science and experimentation into something that might turn a profit. Stubblefield's first invention was a simple tool for lighting coal oil lamps without having to remove the glass chimney. With the help of some local attorneys, he filed a patent application, and a few months later, on November 3, 1885, the Patent Office awarded him the first of four U.S. patents. Unfortunately for Stubblefield, no manufacturer ever produced any of the devices, and none were sold. This is not unusual; only a small fraction of patents ever results in a profitable product. Nevertheless, the experience whetted Stubblefield's appetite for invention.

Stubblefield became fascinated with electricity, which was all the rage in the late 1800s, sort of like computers are today. Besides *Scientific American*, he started reading a new publication called *Electrical World* and learned all about circuits and electrical devices. He built a tiny shack behind the house and used it as a crude laboratory. He also built a library of technical books and manuals.

Stubblefield's hobby soon became an obsession, and he began spending lots of money on electrical equipment and supplies. These expenditures helped push the family into poverty. He was ashamed for being unable to afford decent clothes for his children and, as a result, did not allow them to attend school or church. He was also paranoid about others stealing his ideas. To guard against this imagined threat, he rigged the fences and gates surrounding his property with alarms and always kept a shotgun handy.

In the mid-1880s, Stubblefield focused his attention on telephony. Telephone systems were spreading rapidly across the country, installed mainly by American Bell Telephone, the company that held nearly all the telephone patents. If a rival company wanted to install a telephone system in a community, they would either have to pay a steep franchise fee to Bell Telephone or invent their own equipment in order to avoid infringing on Bell Telephone's patents.

The fiercely independent Stubblefield chose the latter route. In 1885, Stubblefield designed and built a nonelectric, acoustic voice-transmitting device he called a mechanical or vibrating telephone. It worked on the same basic principle as a simple tin can telephone that the reader may have constructed as a child. A tin can telephone comprises two tin cans connected by a tight string or wire. When one speaks into the open end of one can, the sound vibrations are transmitted through the string to the other can. Put your ear to the can, and you hear the voice at the other end. Stubblefield's telephone was more sophisticated and durable—he used wooden sound boxes, for example—but the principle was the same.

Stubblefield's simple telephone had several rather serious drawbacks. First, the wire had to be suspended in air, and wind caused the wire to vibrate. The vibrations caused by the wind interfered with the vibrations produced by a human voice. Thus, the phone could not be used on a windy day. Second, the wire had to be kept taut. This limited the range of the telephone to only a mile. Finally, one of Stubblefield's phones connected to only one other phone; there was no way of switching connections. As a result, customers needed a separate phone and wire for every location they wanted to communicate with.

Despite these limitations, the phone worked reasonably well. Stubblefield sold his first vibrating phone to the Calloway County court clerk in late 1886. Soon, he and his partner, Samuel Holcomb, were selling phones all over western Kentucky and Tennessee, southern Illinois, southeast Missouri and Mississippi. In 1888, Stubblefield was awarded a patent for the design. That same year, Stubblefield came up with an improved version of his telephone that he called the laryngaphone. In this design, the caller could communicate without the sound box by clenching a string with his teeth or by wrapping the string tightly around his neck while talking. The design included an electric bell for better signaling and a hearing tube to improve the volume. Unsurprisingly, the laryngaphone was never patented.

Stubblefield's success with his vibrating phone lasted only about four years. In 1889, a group of Murray business owners formed a company to bring the vastly superior Bell Telephone system to town. Within a year, Stubblefield's vibrating telephone business ended, and he found himself back on the farm.

During the late 1800s (the historical record is not clear about exactly when), Stubblefield began work on his most famous invention, the wireless telephone. Let's be clear about the meaning of wireless telephone. It is wireless in the sense that there is no direct electrical connection through a wire between the telephone transmitter and receiver. Wires are used in the construction of the telephone apparatus, but the actual signal is transmitted through the air, ground or water. If successful, this method would avoid infringing on the patent rights of Bell Telephone, since its system depended on wires to carry the signal.

Stubblefield's first attempt at a wireless telephone was based on a phenomenon known as electromagnetic induction. It's a phenomenon that few people have heard of and even fewer understand, yet it is the basis for our modern electrical civilization. What is it? If you take a loop of wire and change the strength of the magnetic field enclosed by the loop, you create (or induce) a current of electricity in the loop. (Technically, it is more correct to say you need to change the magnetic flux in the loop.) A key word here is change; a constant magnetic field won't work. Adding more loops of wire to make a coil increases the effect, as does increasing the rate of change of the magnetic field. Two scientists working independently—Joseph Henry in the United States and Michael Faraday in England—discovered this phenomenon in 1830.

Before this discovery, the only way to generate electrical current was with a battery. But batteries use expensive chemicals. Electromagnetic induction provides a way of generating electricity without the use of batteries. All you have to do is spin a coil of wire near a magnet (or spin a magnet around a coil of wire) and voilà, you have electricity. This is how electricity is generated on a large scale at electrical power plants. It's all about spinning.

A related effect uses two coils of wire. If one changes the electrical current in one coil of wire (called the primary coil), that creates a changing magnetic field around the coil. If a second coil of wire (called the secondary coil) is placed nearby, it will sense that changing magnetic field and a changing current will also be created in that coil. This is sometimes referred to as an induction circuit. Henry discovered this effect in 1842 at Princeton University. He called it "induction at a distance."

In his first attempt at wireless telephony, Stubblefield used two coils of wire to transmit telephone messages. By 1892, he had constructed a system that he was willing to demonstrate to friends. The details of the apparatus are sketchy because all we have are eyewitness accounts from which we must make guesses. The best-known account comes from Rainey Wells, who, in 1935, related a story of an incident that happened in 1892 when Wells was seventeen. Wells says that Stubblefield invited him out to the farm and took him out to his little shack. He handed him an ordinary telephone receiver attached by wire to a 1,000-turn, one-foot-diameter coil of telephone wire mounted on a wooden keg. He told Wells to walk into the orchard and listen. Stubblefield then spoke into a telephone transmitter that was attached to a wooden box and powered by three 6-volt batteries. A wire from the box ran to a large wire coil, ten feet in diameter with 156 turns, that was wrapped around some trees. Wells clearly heard Stubblefield's voice coming from the receiver saying, "Hello, Rainey. Can you hear me?" Wells was sure that Stubblefield was playing a joke on him and had some wires hidden someplace. But they continued their conversation even as Wells walked around.

Stubblefield continued to experiment with his induction telephone for several years but could never transmit sound more than half a mile. The problem was that to transmit signals over significant distances required gigantic coils and high voltages. This made induction telephones impractical. Stubblefield eventually gave up on induction and went back to the drawing board.

Stubblefield's second attempt at wireless telephony was more successful. The design was based on the fact that earth and water are natural electrical conductors and could therefore take the place of wires. Stubblefield took the battery-powered telephone transmitter he used in the induction telephone, but in place of the coil, he connected it to two iron rods with about fifty feet of telephone wire. The rods were then planted in the ground or immersed in water about one hundred yards apart. He hooked up the telephone receiver to a second pair of rods about a mile from the first. The electrical current on which the sound was encoded would flow from the transmitter to the receiver through the ground or water.

The first public demonstration of Stubblefield's natural conduction wireless telephone took place on New Year's Day 1902 at Murray's courthouse square. Stubblefield's son Bernard assisted with the exhibition and had a set routine of counting to ten, whispering, whistling and playing a harmonica. In front of a crowd of about one thousand witnesses, Bernard broadcast his voice and harmonica music to a set of five receivers scattered around the town, the farthest located five blocks away.

News of what was possibly the world's first wireless broadcast spread quickly. The *Louisville Courier-Journal* published an account the next day, and the *St. Louis Post-Dispatch* sent a reporter to interview the inventor. In the story that appeared in the newspaper, Stubblefield predicted that in the future his device could send news around the country. But the property that made it useful as a broadcasting device made it less useful for its intended purpose as a telephone. The problem was that the ground (or water) conducted the electrical signal in every direction. Anyone with a receiver could hear the message; there was no known way to make the messages private. Stubblefield hoped that he or someone would eventually solve this difficulty.

In March 1902, Stubblefield demonstrated his telephone in Washington, D.C. He did a land test similar to the one he had done in Murray, but this time he also showed off the telephone's use in water. For this demonstration, he rented a small steamer boat that was anchored out in the Potomac River several hundred feet from the shore. He set up a transmitting station in a nearby boardinghouse. Wires extended from the apparatus on the boat and were dropped into the water at the stern. The twenty-five or so passengers on the boat gathered around the three receivers and heard counting, singing and harmonica playing coming from the land-based station. Accounts of the demonstration were reported in the *Washington Times*, the *New York Times* and *Scientific American*.

Stubblefield returned home to Murray with a handful of newspaper clippings but no money. He had not patented his conduction telephone, and the Washington trip had been expensive. He needed investors. Soon, Gerald Fennell, a New York City entrepreneur, came to visit. Fennell had actually met with Stubblefield earlier in the year and told the Kentuckian of his plan to form a company centered on the telephone and solicit investors. At the time, Stubblefield had not agreed to the endeavor. But now Fennell had formed a company called the Wireless Telephone Company of America and offered Stubblefield 500,000 shares of stock in exchange for the exclusive rights to the invention. In addition, Fennell would pay all expenses for Stubblefield and his son to travel to Philadelphia and New York City for a demonstration of the device. Fennell would also handle all the publicity for the events.

Stubblefield agreed to the terms, convinced some friends in Murray to invest in the company and built a new and improved version of the wireless telephone. The first Philadelphia demonstration took place on May 30. It was successful over a maximum distance of a mile and a half and continued through the next week. The next stop for Stubblefield and Bernard was New York City. The site chosen for the demonstration was Battery Park, at the southern tip of Manhattan; it was the park closest to Wall Street. Unfortunately for Stubblefield, his wireless telephone didn't work. Bernard blamed the failure on the rocky soil, but the most likely cause was interference from the large number of electrical circuits in the densely populated city.

Then Fennell asked Stubblefield to do something dishonest. He suggested that the inventor secretly bury wires connecting the transmitter with the receiver so that the wireless telephone would work. Stubblefield was already suspicious about the business. They seemed much more interested in publicity and selling stock than in developing the technology and selling telephone systems. This was the final straw; Stubblefield severed his ties to the company and would have nothing more to do with it. Although the company now had control of Stubblefield's wireless telephone, the technology led nowhere, and the business went under in 1903.

Stubblefield returned to Murray and his wireless induction telephone. In 1908, he patented an induction telephone that could communicate with moving vehicles. One coil would be suspended above the side of the roadway, while the other coil hung from the top of the vehicle. The system worked, but the problem was that the coils had to be within fifty feet of each other. This meant that a series of coils had to run all the way down the street. Alas, Stubblefield sold none of the telephones and made no further progress in telephony.

Stubblefield was now financially desperate and tried to make some money by opening a school on his farm. He called the institution Telephondelgreen and claimed that it "turns everything to gold it touches. Great institution." Stubblefield had home-schooled his own children, so he felt comfortable in the role of schoolmaster. He wrote out a curriculum that included, along with standard grammar school subjects, classes in penmanship, Bible reading, agriculture and fruit growing. As one might expect, there was also a heavy emphasis on science and technology. Stubblefield's school was a complete failure; there is no evidence that any student, aside from his own children, ever enrolled in the school.

In his later years, Stubblefield descended further into paranoia and poverty. His stepmother had purchased part of the farm for Stubblefield, but she kept the deed in her name and later willed it to Stubblefield's three eldest children. The children sold it as soon as they were old enough, leaving Stubblefield with nothing. His wife had had enough of his eccentric behavior and left him. Stubblefield spent the last decade of his life in abject poverty, moving from place to place around Murray. He died on March 28, 1928, although his body, which had been gnawed by rats, wasn't discovered until March 30. According to most accounts, the cause of death was malnutrition, but according to the coroner, he died from heart disease. They buried him in an unmarked grave in the Bowman family cemetery in Murray.

After Stubblefield died, a *New York Times* obituary stated he had "made great strides in what he called 'wireless telephony' and which has become radio." This is perhaps the origin of the myth that Stubblefield had something to do with the invention of radio. He did not. Radio waves are electromagnetic waves consisting of oscillating electric and magnetic fields. They are part of the electromagnetic spectrum, a range of waves that also include gamma rays, X-rays, ultraviolet waves, visible light, infrared waves and microwaves. Radio waves occupy the long wavelength, low-frequency end of the spectrum. Stubblefield never generated radio waves and therefore did not invent radio. His induction telephone used magnetic fields; his natural conduction telephone system sent electricity through the ground. In both cases, he did, in a sense, "broadcast" voice and music over short distances, but not by radio. At best, we can say that Stubblefield made some modest contributions to wireless communication. That's what he did, and it's enough. For a Kentucky farmer working by himself with no academic connections and very little funding, Stubblefield's accomplishments are impressive. He ended up with four U.S. patents but never got a patent on the conduction telephone, his most important invention.

Nevertheless, Murray has been declared the "birthplace of radio," and the town's first radio station was named WNBS after Nathan Beverly Stubblefield. The Kentucky General Assembly was even persuaded to issue a proclamation that Stubblefield was the "father of radio." Sadly, Stubblefield's actual contributions to wireless communications have been overshadowed by a myth.

JOHN THOMPSON

1860–1940

Field | Invention
Major Contribution | Inventor of the Thompson submachine gun
Kentucky Connection | Born in Newport

> I have given my valedictory to arms, as I want to pay more attention now to saving human life than to destroying it. May the deadly T.S.M.G. [Thompson submachine gun] always "speak" for God and Country. It has worried me that the gun has been so stolen by evil men and used for purposes outside our motto, "On the side of law and order."
>
> —Thompson near the end of his life, quoted in the book Tommy: The Gun That Changed America, by Karen Blumenthal

JOHN TALIAFERRO THOMPSON was born in Newport, Kentucky, on New Year's Eve 1860. His mother was Maria Taliaferro, whose Italian last name had been anglicized and was pronounced "Toliver." His father was James Thompson, a lieutenant colonel in the army who was soft-spoken but also a strict disciplinarian. An 1851 graduate of West Point, Lieutenant Colonel Thompson fought in the Battles of Glendale and Chickamauga during the Civil War on the Union side. James retired from the military in 1869 and taught military science at Indiana University until his death in 1880.

John Thompson grew up on military posts in Kentucky, Tennessee, Ohio and California. At age sixteen, he decided on a military career. He attended a preparatory high school in Bloomington, Indiana, and won an appointment to West Point where he graduated in 1882, ranking eleventh in his class. That same year, Thompson married Juliet Estelle Hagans; a year later, their only child, Marcellus Hagans Thompson, was born. Thompson's first military assignment was to the Newport Barracks back in Kentucky. He attended engineering and artillery school and became a specialist in small arms. In 1890, he was assigned to the U.S. Army's Ordnance Department, where he would spend the rest of his military career.

In 1898, the Spanish-American War broke out. Thompson was sent to Tampa, Florida, where he, as chief ordnance officer, was responsible for getting weapons from Tampa to the battle area in Cuba. When he arrived in late April, a logistical nightmare welcomed him. Supply trains were backed up for fifty miles, guns and ammunition were arriving in unmarked boxes and invoices would show up days before or after the shipments. But Thompson would bring order to the chaos and oversaw the efficient delivery of eighteen thousand tons of munitions to Cuba with no accidents. The feat earned Thompson a promotion to colonel.

During this time, an event took place that would steer Thompson toward the invention of his submachine gun. Fifteen hand-cranked Gatling guns that nobody seemed to know what to do with had arrived in Tampa—no orders had been issued regarding their use. Second Lieutenant John Parker suggested to Thompson that the weapons be used to create a Gatling gun unit. The two men agreed the army should modernize its battlefield weapons, especially regarding rapid-fire automatic guns. At the time, the army brass considered such weapons as battlefield accessories rather than central weapons of war. They were "weapons of emergency" to be used only in special situations. In fact, the army's drill instructions in 1911 stated that "fire alone cannot be depended upon to stop an attack." If successful in battle, a Gatling gun unit might convince the army to develop new automatic weapons.

Thompson put Parker in charge of the guns, gave him some ammunition and helped him secretly ship everything to Cuba. Parker didn't disappoint; his little unit played a big role in the famous Battle of San Juan Hill on July 1, 1898. The Gatling guns provided cover while Colonel Theodore Roosevelt and his Rough Riders stormed the Spanish positions. The battle earned Parker the nickname "Gatling Gun" Parker. Thompson's experience with the Gatling guns piqued his interest in automatic weapons and in the small arms used by average combat soldiers.

After the war, Thompson was appointed chief of the Small Arms Division of the Ordnance Department. In 1904, Thompson and Colonel Louis A. La Garde were tasked with finding the caliber of bullet best suited for handgun ammunition. In the Philippine-American War of 1899–1902, the .38-caliber bullet issued to soldiers could not stop enemy combatants. One story told of an escaped prisoner who was shot four times with a .38 and kept running until he was stopped after being hit by the butt of a rifle. The army needed a bullet soldiers could depend on.

As part of their tests, Thompson and La Garde fired shots into live cattle at a Chicago slaughterhouse and into human cadavers from medical schools. They found that large, slower-moving bullets of about .45 caliber were more destructive than smaller bullets moving at a higher speed. Thompson then helped develop the .45-caliber rimless cartridge that were later used in his submachine gun.

When World War I erupted in 1914, the United States remained neutral, although it supplied the Allied forces with weapons and material. Thompson was sympathetic to the Allied cause and was weary of trying to convince the army of the need to adopt automatic weapons. He saw an opportunity to make a difference in the war and earn a larger paycheck for himself. To the surprise of everyone at the Ordnance Department, Thompson retired from the army and went to work for the Remington Arms Corporation. His job was to run what at the time was the world's largest rifle factory, the Eddystone Arsenal in Chester, Pennsylvania. The factory eventually produced two thousand rifles every day for the British and Russian armies.

With the financial backing of a rich investor, in August 1916, Thompson created the Auto-Ordnance Company based in Cleveland, Ohio. The company's goal was to manufacture weapons designed by Thompson. As World War I progressed, Thompson realized that trench warfare required a new type of weapon. The problem was that the enemy had a new weapon called a machine gun. It required three or four soldiers to operate but could mow down soldiers who had to run across the battlefield to mount an attack. The standard-issue rifles used by the Allies had to be manually reloaded after firing and were no match for the machine guns. Thompson came up with the idea of a "trench broom," a weapon that would allow a single soldier to clear an enemy trench using a rapidly firing automatic gun. The new gun would give ordinary soldiers a fighting chance against the ferocious machine guns. Thompson and his engineers got to work on the new weapon—a hand-held portable machine gun.

After months of searching for a suitable design, Thompson discovered a new type of breech lock that he thought would work for his gun. (A breech lock confines the high-pressure gas released when a gun is fired to the barrel of the gun. Otherwise, the gas could damage the weapon or injure the shooter.) The breech lock was invented by a retired naval commander named John Blish. In exchange for stock in the Auto-Ordnance Company, Blish agreed to transfer the patent to Thompson.

Once a prototype was ready, Thompson put it to the test. But after firing only a few rounds, the mechanism jammed. It turned out that the ammunition, rifle cartridges, was too high-powered, resulting in a damaged breech lock. This was potentially a fatal flaw, but Thompson's chief engineer saw a simple solution: use less powerful ammunition. So they switched from a high-powered rifle cartridge to a lower-powered .45-caliber pistol cartridge. It worked. But now Thompson faced another major problem. Machine guns used a long belt of ammunition, but Thompson's gun had to be portable. Thompson solved the problem by replacing the long belt with a large, circular magazine. (A magazine holds the ammunition and feeds it into the firing chamber.) A final problem, overheating, was solved by placing ridges along the gun barrel; the larger surface area would allow heat to escape more quickly.

The gun, just shy of two feet long, featured two grips, one for each hand, and a circular magazine holding one hundred rounds of .45-caliber ammunition. It was designed for use at close quarters, could be fired from the shoulder or the hip and could shoot several hundred bullets every minute. The gun was not very accurate, but it was lightweight (just twelve pounds fully loaded), easy to use and cheap to make. Why is it called a submachine gun? Because a machine gun fires large rifle ammunition, whereas a submachine fires smaller handgun ammunition. Thus, a submachine gun has considerably less firepower than a machine gun.

The first Thompson submachine guns were sitting on the docks, ready to be shipped in December 1918. But the war was over, and Thompson's weapon was not used in battle. Unfortunately for Thompson, the military no longer had a need for the gun. He tried to sell the weapon to law enforcement agencies, but by 1928, low sales had brought the Auto-Ordnance Company to a financial crisis. Thompson was replaced as head of the business.

Nevertheless, the Thompson submachine gun became one of the most iconic weapons in history. It became the weapon of choice for organized crime during the Prohibition era and was a common sight in newsreels and gangster films. The Thompson submachine gun's best-known nickname was

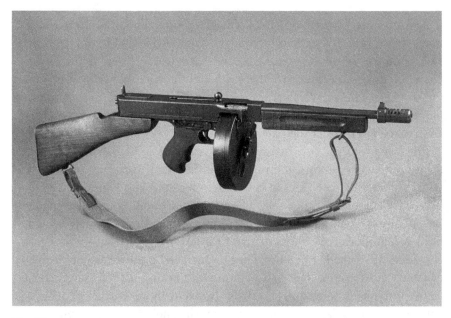

The Thompson submachine gun with the round drum magazine. *Shutterstock.*

The John Thompson House at 24 Third Street in Newport, Kentucky, is now a performance venue. *Wikimedia Commons.*

John Thompson
holding his
submachine gun.
Wikimedia Commons.

the "Tommy Gun," but it was also known by other colorful names, including the "Street Sweeper," the "Annihilator," the "Chicago Typewriter," the "Chicago Piano" and the "Chicago Organ Grinder." Criminal use of the gun continued through the 1920s and '30s, prompting lawmakers to enact the National Firearms Act of 1934, a bill that required certain firearms to be registered and taxed. The $200 tax, equivalent to nearly $3,900 in today's dollars, was intended to make the cost of the guns prohibitive. In 1938, with World War II looming, the U.S. military began using the Thompson submachine gun. During that conflict, over 1.5 million Thompson submachine guns were produced.

Alas, John T. Thompson didn't live to see his weapon used in a war. He died of a heart attack at age seventy-nine on June 21, 1940, in Long Island, New York. He was buried at the United States Military Academy at West Point. Thompson's house at 24 East Third Street in Newport, Kentucky, built in the early 1800s, is marked as a historical site. The large house, more like a mansion, now serves as a venue for musical acts.

THOMAS HUNT MORGAN

1866–1945

Field | Genetics

Major Contribution | Won the Nobel Prize in Physiology or Medicine in 1933 for his discoveries concerning the role played by the chromosome in heredity

Kentucky Connection | Born and raised in Lexington, graduated from the University of Kentucky

> *That the fundamental aspects of heredity should have turned out to be so extraordinarily simple supports us in the hope that nature may, after all, be entirely approachable. Her much-advertised inscrutability has once more been found to be an illusion due to our ignorance. This is encouraging, for, if the world in which we live were as complicated as some of our friends would have us believe we might well despair that biology could ever become an exact science.*
>
> —*Morgan in* The Physical Basis of Heredity

THOMAS HUNT MORGAN was born into a distinguished family on September 25, 1866, in Lexington. His father, Charlton Hunt Morgan, served as U.S. consul to Sicily, returning in 1861 to join his brother, General John Hunt Morgan, in the Confederate army. Charlton was captured several times and wounded at the Battle of Shiloh. He was related to businessman J.P. Morgan. Thomas's mother, Ellen Key Howard, was from a well-to-do Baltimore family. Her two grandfathers were John Eager Howard, a former governor of Maryland, and Francis Scott Key, composer of the national anthem. The family ran a Lexington hemp factory.

As a boy, Morgan was fascinated by natural history. He spent several summers in Oakland, in extreme western Maryland, where he wandered the mountains hunting fossils and collecting bird eggs. When he was older, he was employed in the summer doing biological and geological fieldwork in the mountains of Kentucky. At age sixteen, he matriculated to what was then Kentucky State College (now the University of Kentucky), where he majored in zoology.

He earned his degree in 1886, graduating as valedictorian, and spent the summer at a marine laboratory in Annisquam, Massachusetts. In the fall, he began graduate studies at Johns Hopkins University, a new institution founded just ten years earlier in Baltimore. A letter written late in his life explains that Morgan was attracted to Johns Hopkins "by the rather vague rumors that reached us as undergraduate students in far distant colleges. In my own case it was through Joseph Castle who had preceded me by a couple of years. Perhaps the fact that my mother's family were Baltimoreans had some effect; but little did I know then how little they appreciated that a great university had started in their midst."

At Johns Hopkins, Morgan studied morphology, the study of the structure of living organisms, and physiology, the study of the functions and mechanisms within a living organism. Morgan was also introduced to the field of embryology, a branch of biology that studies embryos and fetuses. Morgan earned his doctorate in 1890 after writing his dissertation on the embryology of sea spiders, concluding that their development was more closely related to spiders than to crustaceans. He had collected sea spider specimens during the summer at the Marine Biological Laboratory at Woods Hole in Massachusetts (now the Woods Hole Oceanographic Institute), a place he would return to nearly every summer until his twilight years. After graduating, Morgan was awarded the Adam Bruce Fellowship, which provided financial support for further study and research. He spent the next year traveling to Jamaica, The Bahamas and Europe, where he did research at the Marine Zoological Laboratory in Naples, Italy.

In 1891, Morgan was hired as a professor at Bryn Mawr College, a new all-female school near Philadelphia, where he taught the morphology-related courses, lecturing twice each day, five days a week. Morgan was an enthusiastic teacher, but he was more interested in research. During his first several years at Bryn Mawr, he did descriptive research on sea acorns, worms and frogs. During the 1894–95 academic year, Morgan took a leave of absence and returned to Naples, where his research shifted toward experimental embryology. In 1895, he returned to Bryn Mawr, where his main areas of research were larval development and regeneration, the ability of some organisms to replace missing tissue.

Thomas Hunt Morgan, shown here in 1891, won the Nobel Prize for Medicine or Physiology in 1933 for his discoveries in genetics. *Wikimedia Commons.*

During the summer of 1891 at Woods Hole, Morgan was introduced to a student named Lilian V. Sampson, who had just graduated with honors from Bryn Mawr. She had won a fellowship to continue her studies at the University of Zurich, but she returned to Bryn Mawr in the fall of 1892 to work on her master's degree. With Morgan serving as her advisor, she finished her degree in the spring of 1894. The student and the professor must have enjoyed working together, because ten years later, in 1904, the two married.

The couple moved to New York City, where Morgan, who had built a solid reputation for experimental research, had accepted a position at Columbia University. Lilian put her scientific career on hold to raise a family. She also took on the responsibility of handling their household and personal affairs, allowing Morgan to concentrate on his research, a key factor in Morgan's subsequent success. It would be sixteen years before she published another scientific paper. The couple had four children: Howard Key (1906), Edith Sampson (1907), Lilian Vaughan (1910) and Isabella Merrick (1911). The family spent summers at Woods Hole, where Lilian kept a summer home that served as a residence for relatives and graduate students. In 1913, Sampson and several other women founded the Summer School Club at Woods Hole (now the Children's School of Science).

It was at Columbia that Morgan did his most important work, which requires a little historical context to understand and appreciate. By the early 1900s, scientists understood the cell was the basic building block of living organisms. Moreover, when cells divide, scientists observed little threadlike structures in the cell that doubled in number and then migrated to each of

The campus of Columbia University in New York City. *Shutterstock*.

the daughter cells. They called these chromosomes, discovered around 1880. But the function of the chromosomes was unknown, although by the turn of the century it was hypothesized that they carried genetic information.

The science of genetics began with the discoveries of Gregor Mendel, an Austrian monk who experimented with pea plants. Beginning in 1856, Mendel bred peas with seven pure properties such as color, size, shape and texture. Then he cross-bred peas with different traits: tall with short, smooth with wrinkled and so on. He expected to get a blend of the characteristics: medium height, partially smooth and so on. Instead, he found some plants grew tall and some grew short, some were wrinkled and others were smooth. The traits had been inherited independently of one another.

Mendel also found that traits were inherited in particular ratios. Take seed color, for example. Mendel found that when a yellow pea and a green pea were crossbred, the first-generation offspring always produced yellow peas. The green peas reappeared in the second generation in a ratio of three yellow to one green. To account for this pattern, Mendel invented the terms dominant and recessive and applied them to different traits. In the seed color example, yellow would be the dominant trait and green the recessive. In 1866, Mendel published his results, which showed the actions of what he called invisible "factors" in determining the traits of organisms. The papers were ignored until they were rediscovered in 1900.

Morgan used fruit flies (*Drosophila melanogaster*) to study genetics. Fruit fly research has led to five Nobel Prizes. *Shutterstock.*

But Morgan didn't believe Mendel's results. In a 1909 speech titled "What Are 'Factors' in Mendelian Explanations," Morgan poked fun at Mendel's mysterious "factors": "In the modern interpretation of Mendelism, facts are being transformed into factors at a rapid rate. If one factor will not explain the facts, then two are invoked; if two prove insufficient, three will sometimes work out." Morgan decided to investigate inheritance himself, thinking that he would disprove Mendel's findings.

A visit to the garden of Hugo de Vries in the Netherlands had piqued Morgan's interest in genetics. Looking at the myriad varieties of flowers, it occurred to Morgan that maybe mutation was the driver of evolutionary change.

In 1907, Morgan began experimenting with the common fruit fly, the scientific name of which is *Drosophila melanogaster*, to investigate this possibility. Why fruit flies? First, they are small and cheap and don't take up much room—an important consideration in a cramped laboratory. Second, flies require minimal care; just stick them in a little jar, throw in a piece of fruit and they'll be happy. Third, they have just four unusually large chromosomes, making them easy to study. Finally, the flies bred quickly, producing a new generation in just twelve days.

Morgan's tiny lab, in room 613 of Schermerhorn Hall at Columbia University, measured just sixteen feet by twenty-three feet. It held eight desks and thousands of flies housed in quart-sized milk bottles that, according to legend, his assistants "borrowed" from the cafeteria and the stoops of apartment buildings. A bunch of rotting bananas hung from the ceiling to attract the fruit flies. The lab became affectionately known as the "fly room." (Today, the former fly room space is occupied by a prep area for the undergraduate biology labs.)

For the first couple of years, Morgan had little to show for his work with flies. The breakthrough came in 1910, when he noticed that one of his flies had white eyes rather than the usual red. Over the next several months, he bred the fly and its descendants and monitored the results. He was so completely absorbed by his work that, according to a story told in Ronald Clark's book *The Survival of Charles Darwin*, he visited his wife just after she had given birth and immediately began a rather long-winded lecture on

The entrance to Columbia's Schermerhorn Hall where Morgan's fly lab was located. *Shutterstock.*

the exploits of the white-eyed fly. Upon finishing, he asked, almost as an afterthought, "And how is the baby?"

The baby was fine, and the fly experiments began yielding results. After breeding the original white-eyed fly, Morgan found that the first-generation progeny were all red-eyed. But in the second generation, the white eyes reappeared. The ratio of red eyes to white eyes was three to one, exactly what Mendel had found in his pea plant experiments. As a scientist, Morgan had to be led by the evidence—Mendel was right after all. Equally important was the fact that all the white-eyed flies were male. This showed to Morgan that the white-eyes trait was linked to sex, a phenomenon known as gene linkage. He had proven that genes were physical entities located along the chromosomes. David DePew and Bruce Weber, in their book *Darwinism Evolving*, called Morgan's work "some of the most beautiful experimental results in the history of science."

But Morgan was not finished. He developed what later became known as the chromosomal theory of inheritance and created much of the language of genetics. He identified genetic processes and mechanisms including assortment, recombination and segregation. The work was summarized in several books, including *Heredity and Sex* (1913), *The Mechanism of Mendelian Heredity* (1915), *The Physical Basis of Heredity* (1919), *Embryology and Genetics* (1924), *Evolution and Genetics* (1925), *The Theory of the Gene* (1926) and *Experimental Embryology* (1927). All these texts are now considered classics in the field of genetics.

In summary, Morgan proved that genes are segments of chromosomes. Traits related to one another have genes that lie close to each other on the chromosomes. And he discovered that parts of different chromosomes can trade places with one another. For his discoveries in genetics, Morgan was awarded the Nobel Prize in Physiology or Medicine in 1933. Morgan had not worked alone; several graduate students labored alongside Morgan in his fly room. Most notable among these were Alfred Sturtevant, Calvin Bridges and Hermann Joseph Muller. In recognition of the group effort, Morgan gave his prize money to his own children and to the offspring of Bridges and Sturtevant. (Muller, who left the Columbia lab in 1920, won his own Nobel Prize in 1946.) Morgan did not attend the Nobel Prize award ceremony in 1933. Instead, he attended in 1934 and gave a speech in which he wrongly predicted that genetics would not significantly contribute to medicine. Morgan wasn't right all the time.

After the children were deemed old enough, Lilian Morgan returned to the laboratory to study fruit fly genetics. The family could financially afford servants, and this no doubt played a role in her return to research. According to their daughter Isabella, her father "made it clear to her that in the laboratory she would be on her own, an independent investigator in no sense an assistant to him." Morgan gave his wife some working space in the fly room, but she held no official position. She was in the somewhat awkward position of being the spouse of the head of the lab, and her husband was never completely comfortable with her presence. She was never part of the inner circle, which consisted of Morgan, Sturtevant, Bridges and Muller. There were a few other women in the lab, but they were much younger than Lilian, and Mrs. Morgan was not outgoing or talkative. All these factors added to her isolation. One woman working in the lab in 1925 described the atmosphere as "a little like that of an exclusive men's club." Yet Lilian carried on with her research and made a few significant discoveries of her own. Such were the times.

Morgan eventually gave up his fly research and returned to topics that he loved, most notably marine animals. Fruit fly genetics had become too complex for Morgan, who was not an adept mathematician. He passed the fruit fly baton to his capable students. Over time, five more Nobel Prizes would be awarded to other scientists for research involving fruit flies.

After twenty-five years at Columbia, Morgan was within a few years of retirement when, in 1927, he was offered a position at the California Institute of Technology. The offer came directly from George Ellery Hale, the famous telescope builder and now president of the school, who wanted Morgan to reorganize the biology department. Morgan accepted the offer and moved to Pasadena in 1928, bringing along Sturtevant, Bridges and other Columbia faculty. Although Morgan's best years as a scientist were behind him, he set to work building Caltech's biology program with an emphasis on genetics, evolution, embryology, physiology, biochemistry and biophysics. Morgan fostered an atmosphere that encouraged interactions between biologists, chemists and physicists.

Norman Horowitz, a Caltech geneticist who knew Morgan during his later years, says his favorite story from those days was when Morgan got a visit from the famous English writer H.G. Wells. Horowitz saw Wells at the entrance to the biology building, all dressed up in a white suit, Panama hat, spats and a cane. Morgan came out in his usual wrinkled and out-of-style attire. Morgan then took Wells on a tour. One could hear exactly where they were in the building because Morgan, who was hard of hearing, assumed that anyone his age would have a similar problem and therefore spoke to Wells in a very loud voice. Horowitz also remembered that at the weekly biology seminars, Morgan would introduce the speaker and then take his seat in the front row next to his wife, Lilian. Before the speaker had completed his second sentence, Morgan was usually asleep. Lilian would then nudge him and whisper, "Tom! Tom!" into his ear. After his little catnap, Morgan would wake up refreshed and often had an interesting question for the speaker at the conclusion of the talk.

Morgan also played an important role in the American eugenics movement. Eugenics, the idea that humanity could be improved through selective breeding, was a popular movement in the early 1900s. Morgan jumped on the bandwagon by joining the board of the Eugenics Record Office (ERO) at Cold Spring Harbor on Long Island in 1910. The ERO was a research institute that collected biological and social information on the American population and was the center for the eugenics movement. But after his research on fruit flies, it became clear to Morgan that the mechanism of heredity was much more complicated than previously thought. Morgan argued that because the eugenicists did not clearly define the traits they were trying to manipulate, the genetic basis of the traits could not be correctly determined. He also argued that intellectual and behavioral traits were not completely hereditary and could be caused by cultural and social conditions. Therefore, eugenics should not be the basis for writing laws. Morgan left the movement after 1915 and became a vocal opponent and influential critic. By 1939, the eugenics movement in America was over.

As is true of many scientists, Morgan was not religious. In a reminiscence about Morgan's Caltech days, Horowitz had this to say: "Morgan's passion for experiment was symptomatic of his general skepticism and his distaste for speculation. He believed only what could be proven. He was said to be an atheist, and I have always believed that he was. Everything I knew about him—his skepticism, his honesty—was consistent with disbelief in the supernatural."

Morgan finally retired from Caltech in 1942 but kept an office across the street from the biology department and continued his research. Morgan died on December 4, 1945, at age seventy-nine, from a heart attack. A year after his death, Morgan's wife, Lilian, was appointed, at age seventy-six, a research assistant at Caltech, her first official position. Morgan's last scientific paper appeared in the *Journal of Experimental Zoology* in the same month he died. The Thomas Hunt Morgan School of Biological Sciences at the University of Kentucky is named in his honor. One of Morgan's students, Alfred Sturtevant, described his personality as "enthusiasm combined with a strong critical sense, generosity, open-mindedness, and a remarkable sense of humor." Nobel Prize winner Eric Kandel wrote: "Much as Darwin's insights into the evolution of animal species first gave coherence to nineteenth-century biology as a descriptive science, Morgan's findings about genes and their location on chromosomes helped transform biology into an experimental science." Thomas Hunt Morgan is arguably the greatest scientist ever to hail from the Bluegrass State.

GARRETT MORGAN

1877–1963

Field | Invention
Major Contribution | Invented hair products, a fire safety hood and a
traffic signal
Kentucky Connection | Born and raised in Claysville, Kentucky, where
he lived until age fourteen

*I am not a well-educated man; however, I have a Ph.D.
from the school of hard knocks and cruel treatment.*

—Morgan in a letter to the mayor of Cleveland
following the Lake Erie Crib Disaster

GARRETT AUGUSTUS MORGAN was born in Claysville, Kentucky, on
March 4, 1877. His father, a former slave named Sydney Morgan, was the
son of Confederate colonel John Hunt Morgan and an unknown enslaved
woman. His mother, a preacher's daughter named Eliza Reed Morgan, was
part Native American. He was the seventh of the couple's eleven children
and spent his childhood helping on the family farm. His formal education
was limited to the sixth grade.

In 1891, at age fourteen, Morgan left home and moved to Cincinnati
in search of work. He found employment as a handyman for a landowner
and used the money he earned to hire a tutor and further his education. In
1895, he moved to Cleveland, where he lived the rest of his life. Morgan was
briefly married to Madge Nelson from 1896 to 1898.

At the turn of the twentieth century, Cleveland was a hub for the garment industry, which employed one out of every seven of the city's residents. Morgan got a job sweeping the floors at the Roots and McBride Company clothing factory for five dollars a week. The company's many sewing machines were often broken down and in need of repair. Morgan taught himself how to fix the cantankerous machines and was soon the company's only Black sewing machine repairman. Not satisfied with merely fixing the machines, his agile mind began thinking about ways to improve them. This led to his first invention: a belt fastener that increased the sewing machine's efficiency. He may have sold the idea for $150 (about $4,300 in today's dollars) although the historical record is not clear. Historians at the Western Reserve Historical Society where Morgan's archives are located say it's likely that Morgan made other improvements to sewing machines that have been lost to history.

In 1907, a competing company offered Morgan a job and he took it. There, he met and fell in love with Mary Hasek, an immigrant seamstress from Bohemia. But there was a problem: he was Black, and she was white. When the company discovered their relationship, it gave the couple a choice: end it or leave. So they left, got married and opened their own children's clothing store. Morgan kept the sewing machines running while Mary made the clothes. Eventually, they opened the Morgan Skirt Factory. The successful businesses earned the Morgans enough money to buy a house on Harlem Avenue in Cleveland. (A historical marker on East Fifty-Fifth Street commemorates the location.)

Morgan's next invention came about because of good luck. He was trying to solve a problem involving the steel needles on the sewing machines. The fast-moving needles got so hot due to friction that they were scorching the fabric. The solution was to lubricate the machinery with oil to reduce the friction. Morgan was experimenting with oils to see which one worked best when, on a lunch break, he wiped his oily hands on a cloth made from hair. When he returned, Morgan noticed that it had straightened the hair on the cloth; the oil must have relaxed the hair fibers. He tested the oil on the curly fur of his neighbor's dog, an Airedale Terrier. It worked. As a final test, Morgan applied the oil to his own hair. Again, it worked. Morgan marketed the product as G.A. Morgan's Hair Refiner and sold it nationwide. According to Morgan's granddaughter Sandra Morgan, it was more popular with men than women because the product gave them a Rudolph Valentino look.

A tragedy inspired Morgan's next invention. On March 25, 1911, a fire engulfed the Triangle Shirtwaist Company in New York City, killing 146 people. Most of the victims were young female garment workers who were trapped inside the building. The incident illustrated the complete inadequacy of the nation's fire codes and safety equipment. Morgan decided to try to do something about it.

Most fire-related deaths come from smoke inhalation, mainly because of carbon monoxide poisoning. Morgan knew that carbon monoxide accumulates at roughly head level and cleaner air sits at floor level. Morgan designed a suit featuring a hose on the backside that hung down near the ground to draw in clean air. The hose split at butt-level with the branches running under the arms and into a hood resembling a beekeeper's helmet. According to Sandra Morgan, the idea for the design came from Morgan watching circus elephants stick their trunks out of hot tents to get some fresh air. The idea was simple, and it worked.

Morgan filed a patent for his "Breathing Device" in September 1912. According to the patent application, the suit would provide a way for a firefighter "to supply himself at will with fresh air from near the floor" and "forcibly remove smoke or injurious gases from the air tube." Later versions included a bag worn on the back that could supply twenty minutes of air. Today, Morgan's device is often compared to a modern gas mask, but the design is closer to a scuba diving suit.

Unfortunately for Morgan, racism hindered the sales of his invention. White fire chiefs refused to buy a product from a Black inventor. Morgan sought advice from one of the world's wealthiest men, J.P. Morgan, and the two Morgans became good friends. J.P. Morgan suggested that Garrett separate himself from the product by dropping the "Garrett A." from the name of the invention and call it the "Morgan National Safety Hood." Morgan followed the advice, and it worked. Morgan later named his first son John Pierpont in honor of his mentor. When J.P. Morgan learned about the naming, he sent the baby a savings bond.

In order to sell his device at firefighter conventions, Morgan hired a white actor to play the role of the inventor. Morgan then donned a costume and posed as the inventor's Native American sidekick named "Big Chief Mason," strapped on the breathing device and fearlessly entered a "teepee" filled with smoke. He exited the tent twenty minutes later in good health. The marketing ploy worked, and sales increased.

In 1916, an accident in Cleveland brought further attention to Morgan's invention. Cleveland was a rapidly growing city, and the sewer system was overwhelmed. To solve the problem, waterwork tunnels extending for miles were dug underneath Lake Erie to provide access to clean water. The workers who built the tunnels were known as "sandhogs" because they had to dig through the sand and limestone. But there was danger lurking beneath the lake in the form of pockets of explosive natural gas. Just before midnight on July 24, 1916, the sandhogs hit a pocket of natural gas four miles offshore and 120 feet below the lake's surface. An explosion occurred, resulting in the deaths of twenty-two workers in what became known as the Lake Erie Crib Disaster. (A crib is an offshore structure that collects fresh lake water for use.)

Garrett Morgan's phone rang at about three o'clock in the morning. He was told about the tragedy and asked if he could assist in the rescue by bringing the breathing device that rescuers had read about in the newspapers. Morgan jumped out of bed, threw several breathing hoods in his car and rushed to the scene, still wearing his pajamas. Morgan, his brother Frank and a few brave volunteers donned the hoods and descended into the tunnel, searching for survivors. Eventually, Morgan and the rescuers pulled out eight men.

The mayor of Cleveland, Harry L. Davis, was at the scene hailing Morgan as a hero and praising the safety hood as a lifesaver. But the next day, newspaper accounts of the accident ignored Morgan's heroic actions. Others involved in the rescue were given medals and cash bonuses, but not Morgan. Several months later, the Carnegie Hero Fund Commission presented awards to the rescuers. When Morgan didn't receive an award, he wrote an angry letter to Mayor Davis complaining that he hadn't vouched for Morgan's actions. The letter concludes by saying that his treatment was enough "to make me and the members of my race feel [that you] will not give a colored man a square deal." (The Carnegie Hero Fund Commission denies that the decision was racially motivated.) Despite the snub, the episode brought even more attention to Morgan's invention. By 1917, the safety hood had become standard equipment for the army during World War I.

An accident also inspired Morgan's final major invention. In the early 1920s, city streets were a busy jumble of people, horses, carts, carriages and cars. There were few traffic laws and many accidents. One day, Morgan was out with his sons when, at an intersection, there was a violent collision between an automobile and a horse-drawn carriage. A little girl was thrown from the carriage and lay badly injured on the street. Morgan's granddaughter said he talked about the tragic accident until the day he died.

Witnessing the accident motivated Morgan to design a new traffic signal for intersections. Electric traffic lights were already in use; the first had been installed in Cleveland in 1914. But there was an important new feature of Morgan's T-shaped hand-operated signal. Instead of two signals, one for "stop" and one for "go," his design included a "caution" signal. According to the patent application, the signal would stop traffic "in all directions before the signal to proceed in any one direction is given." This would allow the intersection to clear, thus avoiding accidents. Morgan had invented the idea of the yellow light.

Morgan filed a patent for his new three-position traffic signal on February 27, 1922. Afraid that his race might scare off potential customers, the evidence suggests that Morgan sold the patent to the General Electric Company for $40,000 (about $610,000 in today's dollars). General Electric then installed three-armed traffic signals in cities across the country. Presumably, this resulted in the prevention of thousands of accidents and saved many lives.

Morgan became a leader in Cleveland's Black community. He co-founded an African American newspaper named the *Cleveland Call* (later renamed the *Call and Post*). He was active in the city's chapter of the NAACP, donated to Black colleges and ran for the city council. With the money he earned from his inventions, Morgan bought 250 acres in Wakeman, Ohio, about forty-five miles west of Cleveland, where he built an African American country club featuring a party room and a dance hall.

In his later years, Morgan developed glaucoma, and by 1943, he was legally blind. Although he experienced blindness and poor health for the rest of his life, Morgan, who called himself the "Black Edison," continued to invent. Among the last of his creations was a self-extinguishing cigarette, which featured a small plastic pellet of water placed in front of the filter. Garrett Morgan died at the Cleveland Clinic after a lingering illness on July 27, 1963, at age eighty-six. He is buried in Lake View Cemetery in Cleveland.

Today, some of Morgan's inventions are on display at the museums of the Smithsonian Institution. At the Smithsonian's American History Museum, one can see the original wooden prototype of his traffic signal, and at the National Museum of African American History & Culture, a Morgan Safety Hood is on display.

ST. ELMO BRADY

1884–1966

Field | Education
Major Contribution | The first African American to earn a doctorate in chemistry in the United States, he became a leader at several historically Black colleges.
Kentucky Connection | Born and raised in Louisville

Brady not only built buildings and departments, he built men and women. He was never too busy to listen to the problems of a student or fellow faculty member.... Although he is gone as a person, his shadow remains. It will always remain when men turn down offers for personal gain to serve others. It will always be there as a friendly teacher helps a student or a young colleague. It will show wherever better facilities in chemistry are erected....Truly the story of chemistry at four institutions is the lengthened shadow of a great teacher, friend, and scholar—St. Elmo Brady.

—Samuel Massie, African American chemist at the U.S. Naval Academy, in a tribute published in The Capital Chemist *in 1967*

ST. ELMO BRADY was born in Louisville on December 22, 1884, the first of three children of Thomas Alexander Brady and Celester Parker Brady. His unusual name comes from the main character in the novel St. Elmo, a story about the uneasy relationship between the cynical Saint Elmo and a beautiful and devout heroine. It was one of the most popular novels of the nineteenth century, selling a million copies in four months.

Little is known about Brady's childhood. After graduating from Louisville Colored High School in 1903, he went on to Fisk University, a historically Black college in Nashville, Tennessee. There, he met Thomas W. Talley, a chemistry teacher who encouraged Brady to pursue a career in science. He earned his bachelor's degree in 1908 at the age of twenty-four and accepted a teaching position at the Tuskegee Normal and Industrial Institute (now Tuskegee University) in Alabama. At Tuskegee, he was mentored by George Washington Carver, an agricultural scientist famous for his peanut-based inventions and the most prominent Black scientist of the early twentieth century. The university was under the leadership of Booker T. Washington, whom Brady also knew. Brady later wrote, "It was the friendship of these two men that showed me the real value of giving one's self and effort to help the other fellow."

In 1912, the chemistry department at the University of Illinois, among the best in the country, offered Brady a scholarship to graduate school. It was an opportunity he could not refuse. He took a leave of absence from Tuskegee and began studies during the summer of 1913. He earned his master's degree in 1914 and continued working toward a doctorate under the direction of Clarence G. Derick. Brady and Derick published three scholarly abstracts in *Science*, the most prestigious scientific journal in the United States. He also collaborated on a paper with George Beal that was published in the *Journal of Industrial and Engineering Chemistry*. Because of these publications, Brady became, in 1914, the first African American admitted to Phi Lambda Upsilon, the national chemistry honor society. In 1915, he became the first African American to be inducted into Sigma Xi, the national science honor society.

For his doctoral research, Brady was tasked with settling an argument between Derick and Arthur Michael, a chemist at Harvard. The disagreement centered on how the acidity of certain acids was affected by replacing the hydrogen atoms with other chemicals. Specifically, Brady looked at how the acidity changed when a pair of hydrogen atoms were replaced by an oxygen atom. Brady's research supported Derick's view and resulted in new methods for preparing and purifying certain compounds. It was an early contribution to the new field of physical organic chemistry.

Brady wrote up his research in a 228-page dissertation titled "The Scale Influence of Substituents in Paraffine Monobasic Acids. The Divalent Oxygen Atom." He gave a successful oral defense of his work on May 22, 1916, and became the first African American to earn a doctorate in chemistry in the United States. In November 1916, he was featured as the "Man of the Month" in *The Crisis*, the monthly magazine of the NAACP. Years later, Brady told his students that when he went to graduate school at Illinois, "they began with twenty whites and one other, and ended in 1916 with six whites and one other." He was the "one other"—a Black man.

After earning his doctorate, Brady returned to Tuskegee in the fall of 1916, where he resumed his teaching career. He served as the head of the Division of Science, developed the chemistry program and published a book titled *Household Chemistry for Girls*. At Tuskegee, Brady met and dated an English teacher named Myrtle Marie Travers. The couple married on August 28, 1917, and had two sons, St. Elmo Brady Jr. and Robert Brady. For a period during their marriage, Brady and his wife lived apart, because after Myrtle left Tuskegee, she refused to move back to the South. The couple kept their marriage together by writing letters in which they always addressed each other as "My Dear Sweethearty."

In 1920, Brady accepted a position at Howard University in Washington, D.C., where he eventually became chairperson of the chemistry department. There, he helped establish the first graduate program in chemistry at a historically Black college. He also helped raise funds for a new chemistry building.

Before work on the new building began, Brady returned to Fisk University in 1927, where he remained for twenty-five years until his retirement in 1952. At Fisk, Brady developed the undergraduate chemistry curriculum, assembled an outstanding chemistry faculty and taught general and organic chemistry. In honor of his mentor, Brady started the Talley Lectures, where famous chemists from around the country were invited to visit the campus and give a talk. He got funding to purchase one of the country's first infrared spectrophotometers and, in collaboration with the University of Illinois, began the Infrared Spectroscopy Institute, a summer program open to college faculty that provided training in the subject. Brady also continued his own research program at Fisk, which resulted in several publications.

Brady was also responsible for the construction of a new chemistry building on the Fisk campus. The building opened in 1931 just four years after Brady's arrival and five years before the chemistry building back at Howard was finished. Thus, it became the first modern chemistry building at a historically Black college. Today, the building is known as Talley-Brady Hall and is listed on the National Register of Historic Places. The 36,500-square-foot building houses classrooms, laboratories and offices.

Brady retired from Fisk in 1952, but Tougaloo College in Mississippi recruited him to help organize their chemistry department. For the next fourteen years, Brady worked to build yet another department. He set to work hiring excellent faculty and constructing a new chemistry building. He also continued his own research program in which he studied chemical substances from privet plants with the elusive goal of developing a cancer and malaria treatment from privet berries.

St. Elmo Brady, scientist, educator and builder of chemistry departments, died on Christmas Day 1966 at age eighty-two. In a ceremony at the University of Illinois on February 5, 2019, the American Chemical Society honored Brady with a plaque designating the spot as a National Historic Chemical Landmark. Identical plaques sit at the four historically Black colleges where Brady worked. The plaques read:

In 1916, St. Elmo Brady (1884–1966) became the first African-American to obtain a Ph.D. in chemistry in the U. S. for dissertation work with Professor Clarence G. Derick at the University of Illinois at Urbana-Champaign. Brady went on to a research career in organic chemistry and served in leadership roles at Tuskegee, Howard and Fisk Universities and at Tougaloo College. He built strong undergraduate chemistry curricula and founded the first graduate chemistry program at a historically black college or university. He was an inspiration to students and colleagues alike during his lifetime, and his courage, determination and impact on others continue to inspire successive generations.

JOHN SCOPES

1900–1970

Field | Education
Major Contribution | Scopes was the defendant in the famous Scopes Monkey Trial in 1925.
Kentucky Connection | Born and raised in Paducah, graduated from the University of Kentucky

> *I had been taught from childhood to stand up for what I thought was right and I did not think the state of Tennessee had any right to keep me from teaching the truth. So I was willing to test the law's constitutionality. If the result has served freedom, then I must give much of the credit to my own parents and to a tolerant environment that taught me early in life to revere truth and love and courage.*

—*from* Center of the Storm: Memoirs of John T. Scopes, 4

JOHN THOMAS SCOPES (known as J.T. to his family) was born in Paducah on August 3, 1900. His father, Thomas Scopes, was born in England, trained as a machinist and came to America in 1885. He eventually settled in Paducah and worked at the giant Illinois Central railroad yard. Although Thomas had a limited education, Scopes said that except for his lawyer, Clarence Darrow, his father was the best-read man he had ever known. By

1840

1881

1854

Charles Darwin, shown in his youth (*left*) in middle age (*right*) and in old age (*middle*). *Shutterstock.*

day, Thomas read Ruskin, Macaulay and Carlyle aloud to his son and, at night, read Mark Twain or Charles Dickens to John and his four sisters until they went to sleep. When Scopes was a little older, his father read aloud passages from Charles Darwin's *Origin of Species*, *Descent of Man* and *The Voyage of the Beagle*. Scopes finished reading Darwin's books himself and concluded that the scientist was correct.

Scopes's mother was Mary Alva Brown, who was born in 1865, just after the Civil War. She had the measles as a child, and the illness affected her vision. Doctors warned her not to strain her eyes, and as a result, her parents removed her from school. So she taught herself to read and write. Of his mother, Scopes said, "In our family she was the business head and the balance wheel, never letting her feelings get out of control, running the home and supporting Dad emotionally so that he could do anything he wanted in the outside world."

Scopes's father was active in the worker's union movement. He attended conventions, gave speeches and held offices at the local level. He was an admirer of socialist leader Eugene Debs and, according to Scopes, "was a socialist in outlook if not in name." And he was also a pacifist who believed that "nothing was settled by war, that both sides lost, that war disrupted homes and society, that its suffering had no meaning, and that those who started wars were not the ones who fought them." Scopes's mother had similar political views, which partially explains why the couple got along so well.

In terms of religion, Scopes's father's views were unorthodox. According to Scopes, "He accepted the teachings and the thought of Jesus without the myths and miracles of Christian dogma. I've often heard him say he didn't believe in a heaven or a hell....He had little patience with many of the professors of organized religion. He thought they were hypocrites."

One particular incident helped form Thomas Scopes's religious opinions and attitudes. He was an elder of the Cumberland Presbyterian Church in Paducah when the other elders shut down the town's red-light district and ran the prostitutes out of town. Thomas was shocked and surprised at their sanctimonious, holier-than-thou attitude. Glaring at his fellow elders, he asked, "What are you going to do about these girls? Are you going to ship them to Mayfield....Or are you going to run them over to Cairo in Illinois?... Have you thought once about what is going to happen to the girls when you get rid of them? They deserve to live and they have to eat, just as we do.... Driving them out-of-town won't solve their problem, nor ours. It won't raise the morality of Paducah. They wouldn't be here as prostitutes in the first place if the men of Paducah hadn't patronized them." Thomas's sermon had no effect, so he left the church and, for the rest of his life, never belonged to another. Over time, Thomas Scopes became an agnostic, although he still believed in the Golden Rule.

John Scopes was clearly a product of his upbringing and family environment. According to Scopes, Clarence Darrow "would have said I had no choice but to stand trial at Dayton and he would have started his proof...with my parents." Scopes's father even claimed that "he was the one on trial for being an independent thinker in a free country." Scopes's family background set the stage for his involvement in the Monkey Trial.

When Scopes was thirteen years old, his dad's work required a move to Danville, Illinois, where the family lived for two years. Another move took them to Salem in southern Illinois, where John finished high school. Ironically, Salem was the birthplace of William Jennings Bryan, who periodically returned to his hometown to give speeches on special occasions. Like his father, John liked to read and spent many happy hours at the

Salem library. Scopes graduated high school in 1919, with Bryan giving the commencement address.

That fall, Scopes entered the University of Illinois at Urbana–Champaign, where he took chemistry from William A. Noyes who "lectured so plainly and simply that I did not bother to buy a text all year." His chemistry lab instructor was John Henry Reedy, who "made every experiment an adventure." Reedy showed Scopes the connection between good teaching and learning. Scopes concluded that: "If the teacher is lively and interesting, he is bound to make his subject lively and interesting—a truth I was to file in my mind for future use, and to profit from."

Unfortunately, in the late spring of 1920, Scopes got sick and was rushed to the university hospital. The doctors thought Scopes had tuberculosis and sent him home. It turned out that Scopes was suffering from a severe case of bronchitis rather than the more serious tuberculosis. He recuperated and, the next fall, thinking a warmer climate might help, transferred to the University of Kentucky (UK). The weather didn't help. Scopes came down with bronchitis again, and by early 1921, he had missed so many classes that he had to drop out. He and a friend, also a dropout, became hobos for a while and traveled around the country on freight trains.

Scopes returned to school in the fall of 1921 and took classes based on the reputation of the professor rather than the name of the course. He ignored degree requirements and took a smattering of classes ranging across the academic spectrum. His interest in science was rekindled by teachers like William Delbert Funkhouser, who "taught zoology so flawlessly that there was no need to cram for the final exam."

As Scopes began his senior year, he discovered that his "pleasant academic wanderings" had resulted in no major or minor. He had taken several law classes, so he majored in law and took classes in geology, child psychology and practice teaching to satisfy the requirements for a minor. Meanwhile, the family had moved back to Paducah, and upon graduating in 1924, Scopes returned home to rest from what had been an exhausting academic year.

Now it was time for Scopes to find a job. In the spring of 1924, he had filed his records with UK's teacher placement bureau. His plan was to earn enough money to return to UK, get his law degree and become an attorney. Near the end of the summer, Scopes got a job offer from Dayton, Tennessee. It was for a science and mathematics teaching position that included coaching football. The position paid $150 a month from September through May. Although Scopes had no experience coaching football, he had played basketball in high school and had solid credentials in science and mathematics. That was good enough for Dayton, and Scopes accepted the job.

Dayton is in Rhea County, Tennessee, about forty miles north of Chattanooga. A small town of about 1,800 people in 1925, Dayton had a furniture store, a mercantile store, two drugstores, a movie theater and the Aqua Hotel. There was a clothing store coincidentally named J.R. Darwin's Everything to Wear Store. The stores were arrayed along the town's single paved L-shaped street. A railroad sliced through town, but trains rarely stopped.

Scopes got a room in the large home of the Bailey family, owners of the hardware store, and soon knew nearly everyone in the small town. Social life centered on the church. Scopes, like everyone else, went to church every Sunday. Teachers were expected to attend services, but Scopes claims he would have gone anyway because there was nothing else to do and no other way to see his friends on Sunday morning.

The most important part of Scopes's job at Rhea County Central High School was coaching the football team. Although he was unprepared for the job, the team was moderately successful and nearly upset the eventual state runner-up. Scopes began teaching his science and math classes in the fall. The school had a tradition of holding weekly assemblies to honor those who had improved life in Dayton. Scopes avoided the assemblies as often as possible by escaping to the basement lab where science classes were taught. Eventually, a few of the high school boys joined him there, where they smoked cigarettes and talked about any subject that appealed to them.

And then it happened. In March 1925, the State of Tennessee passed a law prohibiting the teaching of Darwin's theory of evolution. In his memoir, Scopes makes an interesting comparison between Kentucky's response to laws outlawing the teaching of evolution to Tennessee's reaction. In Kentucky, the controversy resulted from a four- to five-year concerted effort by religious fundamentalists. Before that, the public schools and universities had been teaching evolution for years, with no objections. In 1921, William Jennings Bryan canvased Kentucky making speeches against evolution and in favor of religious fundamentalism. In a speech before a joint session of the Kentucky state legislature on January 19, 1922, Bryan claimed, "They have barred the Bible from the schools—now all I ask is to have this heresy, this anti-Bible teaching, thrown out, too." A few days later, a bill emerged in the Kentucky House of Representatives prohibiting the teaching of "Darwinism, atheism, agnosticism or evolution as it pertains to the origin of man." Two days after the first bill, politicians introduced a similar bill in the state senate.

The bills ignited a statewide debate. Fundamentalist preachers railed against evolution, while ministers from more moderate denominations asserted that there was no conflict between evolution and Christianity. The Episcopal Diocese of Kentucky passed a resolution against the bills. Newspaper editorials across the state argued both for and against the legislation, but the largest newspaper in the state, the *Louisville Courier-Journal*, opposed the bills. Evolution was a hot topic of conversation at many social gatherings.

Most important, educators joined the fight opposing the bills. The president of the University of Kentucky, Frank L. McVey, and science professors W.D. Funkhouser and Glanville Terrell went to the state capitol to lobby against the bills. Legislators were invited to the UK campus to observe what went on in science classes. According to Scopes's memoir, the university leadership employed some sexual politics by choosing the prettiest coeds to guide the tours and dazzle the lawmakers. The goal was to show that the university was doing an outstanding job of educating students and didn't need a state law that would interfere with its efforts.

Humor was also a powerful weapon against the bills. As a joke, one politician introduced a bill requiring that henceforth, water must run uphill. Another bill mandated that the climate and temperature remain pleasant year-round. These bills revealed the ridiculous nature of the anti-evolution bills, and soon, many people were laughing at the proposed legislation.

The organized opposition made the difference, but it was close. The bill was defeated by two votes in the Senate and by a single vote in the House. In Scopes's opinion, Kentuckians themselves were partly responsible for the defeat of the legislation, because in Kentucky, there were three kinds of people:

> *There were the mountaineers who weren't interested in the law.... They didn't bother anyone, and they didn't want anyone bothering them. In central Kentucky, the people practiced a live-and-let-live attitude. In western Kentucky, however, a vocal majority stuck up for the Bible and wanted to force its concept of religion down everybody else's throat. People there thought they had the recipe for heaven and they wanted everyone else to enjoy their good fortune.*

In contrast, Tennessee had no organized opposition to the anti-evolution bills. The University of Tennessee, perhaps afraid of losing funding, didn't fight it. Scopes claimed that in Tennessee, "Most people in high position passed the buck and thereby helped pass the bill. They would have profited by having a Funkhouser or a Terrell in the state." Unopposed, the fundamentalist Christians, led by their standard-bearer William Jennings Bryan, descended on the Tennessee legislature in January 1925. A bill outlawing the teaching of evolution sailed through the House of Representatives on January 28, 1925, by an overwhelming 71–5 vote. In mid-March, the bill passed the senate by a 24–6 margin. On March 21, Tennessee governor Austin Peay signed it into law and claimed, "Probably the law will never be applied. It may not be sufficiently definite to permit of any specific application or enforcement. Nobody believes that it is going to be an active statute." The law became known as the Butler Act after the legislator who introduced the bill.

Austin Peay's benign assessment of the law was sadly mistaken. It only took about a month and a half for the pieces to fall into place for a test case. On Monday, May 4, George Rappelyea, a mining engineer who managed some mining properties in the area, was reading the *Chattanooga Times* when he noticed a story stating that the superintendent of the city's schools had decided against sponsoring a test case. An advertisement by the American Civil Liberties Union offered to pay the expenses of anyone willing to put the anti-evolution law to a constitutional test. Rappleyea reasoned Dayton might be a good place for such a case; it would put the town on the map and be good for business.

The next day, Rappleyea held an informal meeting around a wooden table in Robinson's Drugstore. Fred E. "Doc" Robinson was the pharmacist who owned the drugstore and was also the chair of the Rhea County School Board. Others in attendance were Mr. Brady, who owned the town's other drugstore; Sue Hicks, Dayton's leading lawyer (and the man who may have been the inspiration for the Shel Silverstein song "A Boy Named Sue," popularized by Johnny Cash); Wallace Haggard, another attorney; and someone who worked at the post office. After a discussion, the men pursued Rappleyea's idea and asked Scopes if he would take part in the plan. They sent a young boy to find Scopes and summon him to the drugstore.

Scopes wasn't even supposed to be in Dayton. The school year had ended on May 1, and Scopes had intended to go back to Paducah. Instead, he dawdled in Dayton for a few days for two reasons: an accident and a girl. Two of his students had been injured in a car wreck, and he stayed to look in on them. More importantly, he was interested in a girl whose box of fried chicken would soon be up for auction at an upcoming church social. Scopes wanted to be there to bid on the box.

Scopes was playing tennis when the boy found him and informed him that Mr. Robinson wanted to see him at the drugstore. Scopes assumed Robinson wanted to talk about some school business. He finished the game and walked to the drugstore in his sweat-stained clothes. Robinson offered Scopes a chair at the table, and the soda jerk brought him a fountain drink. Rappelyea began by claiming that biology could not be taught without evolution. Scopes agreed, grabbed a copy of the biology textbook off a shelf (the drugstore supplied the county's textbooks) and showed it to the men.

Scopes was not the regular biology teacher; W.F. Ferguson, the principal, was the biology teacher. But Scopes had filled in for Ferguson during an illness near the end of the school year. Ferguson had been asked to serve as the defendant in the test case but refused. He was married with a family and had too much to lose. Scopes, on the other hand, was a young bachelor. In fact, Scopes wasn't even sure he had taught evolution; he had just reviewed for the final exam. That little technicality didn't stop the men from asking Scopes to serve as a defendant.

Scopes agreed, and Robinson picked up the phone to call the Chattanooga newspaper. He informed the reporter that he was the chair of the school board in Rhea County and that the authorities had arrested a man for teaching evolution. Scopes wasn't actually detained. In fact, he left the meeting at the drugstore and went back to playing tennis. A grand jury indicted Scopes on May 25, and the owner of the *Baltimore Sun* paid the $500 bail. Scopes had no idea the minor scene at the drugstore would lead to a major production at the courthouse.

John T. Scopes, the defendant in the famous Scopes Monkey Trial, was born and raised in Paducah, Kentucky. *Wikimedia Commons.*

The next day, a story appeared in the Chattanooga newspaper about the arrest. Picked up by the Associated Press, the story quickly spread across the nation. The trial was front-page news for about three days and continued to be in the headlines until the end of the proceedings. The most famous reporter to cover the trial was H.L. Mencken, who worked for the *Baltimore Sun.* It was Mencken who labeled the case the "Monkey Trial."

Scopes's legal defense team included attorneys Arthur Garfield Hays, Dudley Field Malone and F.B. McElwee. But the star of the defense team was Clarence Darrow, arguably the greatest criminal lawyer of the twentieth century. Darrow, famous for his defense of killers Leopold and Loeb, was a leading member of the ACLU and an agnostic. Darrow's law partner, W.O. Thompson, also assisted with the defense. Leading the prosecution team was Thomas Stewart, a district attorney who would later become a U.S. senator. He was assisted by Dayton attorneys Gordan McKenzie and Herbert and Sue Hicks. The star of the team was William Jennings Bryan, the three-time Democratic candidate for president, renowned orator and religious fundamentalist.

The story of the trial doesn't really involve Scopes, who was, until the end, merely a spectator. Darrow didn't want to call Scopes as a witness because he was afraid the prosecution would discover that he wasn't the real biology teacher. The details of the famous trial have been written about in numerous books and, except for a few incidents, will not be recounted here. Besides Scopes's own memoir, an excellent account is given in Edward J. Larson's book *Summer for the Gods* (the book's title is a quote about the trial by Clarence Darrow).

In the preface to his memoirs, Scopes says that he sought to correct "small errors of fact and what seem to me larger errors of emphasis" that made their way into some published accounts. The largest error, according to Scopes, concerned what many believe was the dramatic climax of the trial when Clarence Darrow examined Bryan on the witness stand. This episode is certainly the climax of *Inherit the Wind*, the famous play about the trial, later made into a movie. But in Scopes's opinion, Dudley Field Malone, who had served as undersecretary of state during the presidency of Woodrow Wilson, provided the trial's most dramatic moments. Malone's boss, the secretary of state, was William Jennings Bryan. The highlight of the trial, according to Scopes, was the legal argument over whether expert scientific testimony would be admissible as evidence. Bryan argued against it, enjoyed the applause from the audience and sat down thinking he had won the day. Then it was Malone's turn, and he was brilliant. As just a sample of his eloquence, consider this argument:

> *Are we to have our children know nothing about science except what the church says they shall know? I have never seen harm in learning and understanding, in humility and open-mindedness, and I have never seen clearer the need of that learning than when I see the attitude of the prosecution, who attack and refuse to accept the information and intelligence which expert witnesses will give them.*

Malone finished with a flourish:

> *We are ready to tell the truth as we understand it and we do not fear all the truth that they can present as facts. We are ready. We are ready. We feel we stand with progress. We feel stand with science. We feel we stand with intelligence. We feel we stand with fundamental freedom in America. We are not afraid. Where is the fear? We meet it. Where is the fear? We defy it! We ask your Honor to admit the evidence as a matter of correct law, as a matter of sound procedure, and as a matter of justice to the defense in this case.*

Scopes recalls that the courtroom "went wild" after Malone finished. The judge's repeated calls for order in the court were futile. The oration ended a long day in court, and after a few minutes, only three people remained in the room: Bryan, Malone and Scopes. According to Scopes, Bryan said, "Dudley, that was the greatest speech I have ever heard!" Malone responded by saying, "Thank you, Mr. Bryan. I am sorry it was I who had to make it." Malone's eloquent oratory had no effect; the judge ruled against the defense, and no expert witnesses were called. The judge did allow the experts to submit written statements so their evidence could be used in the expected appeal.

As expected, Scopes was found guilty, and the judge imposed a fine of one hundred dollars. At the very end of the trial, Scopes finally made a brief statement, an opportunity he hadn't expected and hadn't prepared for. In response to the judge asking if he had anything to say about why the court should not impose punishment, Scopes said, "Your Honor, I feel that I have been convicted of violating an unjust statute. I will continue in the future, as I have in the past, to oppose this law in any way I can. Any other action would be in violation of my ideals of academic freedom, that is to teach the truth as guaranteed in our Constitution, of personal and religious freedom. I think the fine is unjust." After the defense presented the judge with copies of Darwin's *Origin of Species* and *The Descent of Man*, a benediction was offered, and the great Monkey Trial was over.

The defense appealed the case to the Tennessee Supreme Court, which found that the law was constitutional. However, the court set aside the conviction because of a legal technicality: the jury should have set the fine, not the judge. At the time, Tennessee judges could not impose fines of over $50, and Scopes's fine had been set at $100. In a surprise twist, the court recommended that because Scopes was no longer employed by the state, the

One day, the proceedings were held outside due to the extreme heat. In this photo, Clarence Darrow (*standing*) is interrogating William Jennings Bryan (*seated*). *Wikimedia Commons.*

case should not be pursued any further. This brought an end to the appeals the defense had planned. The Butler Act remained on the law in Tennessee until its repeal in 1967.

Scopes admitted he had one regret at the end of that momentous summer. Because the trial had consumed his time and energy, he never got around to dating the pretty little blonde whose beauty and box of chicken had caused him to linger in Dayton. "The merchants of the town, who had profited the most from the circus, should have given her a vote of thanks," Scopes declared. "She deserves as much credit as anyone for the trial being held in Dayton that summer."

A few days after the trial ended, William Jennings Bryan, still in Dayton, attended a church service, ate an enormous meal, lay down for a nap, had a stroke and died in his sleep. His body was transported by train to Washington, D.C., where he was buried in Arlington National Cemetery. Some people placed the blame for Bryan's death squarely on the shoulders of Clarence Darrow, who put Bryan on the witness stand and subjected him to a withering examination. But according to Scopes, Bryan was his usual exuberant self the day after the famous exchange with Darrow, and he seriously doubted there was any connection between the two events.

Scopes received a mountain of mail after the trial. Overwhelmed, Scopes and some friends took the mostly unopened mail, dumped it in the yard, lit some matches and set the pile on fire. He also received many offers to make money from his notoriety. He turned them all down, hoping to return to a normal life. What was next for Scopes? If the trial hadn't happened, Scopes says he probably would have taught for another year and then returned to the University of Kentucky to pursue a law degree. Or he might have enjoyed teaching and made it his career. Even after the trial, Doc Robinson, president of the school board, offered Scopes his old teaching and coaching job back.

But according to Scopes, "One of my most valued windfalls at Dayton had been listening to and associating with the distinguished scientists.... They had broadened my view of the world and of everything in it." Shortly before the trial was over, Scopes was notified that the expert witnesses had arranged a scholarship fund. He could use the money to pursue graduate study in whatever field he chose. It was an opportunity Scopes couldn't pass up. He told Doc Robinson that he would not be returning to the classroom. Instead, Scopes pursued graduate studies in geology.

Scopes became a student at the University of Chicago because the graduate school had an outstanding reputation and it was closer to Paducah than universities on the East or West Coasts. The scholarship fund would pay for two years of study, enough to complete most of the requirements for a doctorate. Scopes enjoyed his time at Chicago, saying that he "had time to delve into the mysteries of science that I had examined only cursorily as an undergraduate. It was a wide new world and there was fascinating work and intriguing professors."

Scopes continued his friendship with Clarence Darrow, who lived in Chicago. As he was riding the train from Paducah to Chicago in the fall of 1925, Scopes received a telegram instructing him to get off at the Sixty-Third Street Station. The message was signed by Darrow. Scopes spent his first week in Chicago at Darrow's apartment. After that, Scopes saw Darrow nearly every week during his two years of study. Scopes claimed that, except for his father, Darrow had a greater influence on his life than any other person.

Unfortunately for Scopes and members of his family, there were consequences to pay for his involvement in the trial. His sister Lela taught in Paducah schools for six and a half years before attending the University of Kentucky to get her degree. Upon returning to Paducah, she applied for her old job. School officials asked her to state that she did not believe in evolution. She replied she didn't know enough about evolution to come to any conclusion about it and that she thought everyone should have the right to study evolution. Because she refused to deny evolution, her application was rejected. Instead, Lela was hired at a private girl's school in New York. After two years, she accepted a job in Winnetka, Illinois, outside of Chicago, where she taught until she retired. Scopes's younger son Bill later claimed that "despite her trouble in Paducah, Aunt Lela held no grudge, never said anything bad about Paducah or the experience, and even moved back later."

John Scopes also paid a price for the Monkey Trial. The money from his scholarship fund was about to run out, and Scopes needed funding to continue his studies and finish his doctorate. A fellowship was available that could supply the money, and the chair of the geology department recommended Scopes for the honor. The fellowship was offered by what Scopes called "a well-known technical school," but he did not name the institution. A few weeks later, Scopes received a letter from the president of the technical school stating: "Your name has been removed from consideration for the fellowship. As far as I am concerned, you can take your atheistic marbles and play elsewhere." The message, coming from a prominent educator at a highly respected university, shocked Scopes. His dream of earning a doctorate was over, and he chose not to go back into teaching because of his notoriety. He left the academic world and began looking for a job in the private sector.

Scopes got a job with Gulf Oil of South America and moved to Venezuela. He chose fieldwork, and in Venezuela, the "field" meant the jungle. In his two-year adventure in the jungle, Scopes had close encounters with wild animals, indigenous people and pesky insects. In the fall of 1928, Scopes was bitten by bugs and hospitalized for several weeks. After he was treated for blood poisoning, malaria and dysentery, the company sent Scopes home on sick leave.

After Scopes's recovery, Gulf Oil assigned him an administrative job in Maracaibo, Venezuela, where he met his future wife, Mildred Walker, at a country club dance. She was a pretty brown-eyed brunette from South Carolina, the daughter of a construction contractor. She was Catholic, and to please her, Scopes agreed to go along with all the procedures the church required of couples who were to be married in the church. Scopes, an agnostic, politely sat through all the religious instruction and was baptized. The couple married in February 1930. Scopes never became a practicing Catholic.

Shortly after the wedding, Scopes was transferred to the headquarters of Gulf Oil in eastern Venezuela, in the city of Ciudad Bolivar. His new bride went on to New York. An assignment required Scopes to take a boat up the Rio Meta into the neighboring country of Colombia. The problem was that Colombia prohibited Gulf Oil from operating within its borders. The company told Scopes that if the authorities caught him in Colombia, he was to come up with his own reasons for being there; he would have to lie and deny any connection to Gulf Oil.

When Scopes got to the Colombian border, he stopped before crossing. He wanted to think about whether he should actually carry out his illegal and dangerous assignment. He was in charge, so his decision would not affect any colleagues who were with him. Scopes spent several weeks weighing the pros and cons of his situation. He had just recently married; he was risking arrest; he could be thrown in jail and never heard from again. Scopes had never been blindly obedient to anybody, and he didn't intend to start now. He decided that his job with Gulf Oil wasn't worth the risk. He turned the boat around and eventually made his way back to Maracaibo. As expected, Scopes was called in to the chief geologist's office and informed that the company was cutting back on expenses and his services were no longer required, but Scopes was smart enough to know the real reason they had fired him.

Scopes had saved up enough money to return to the University of Chicago and finish work on his doctorate. Before leaving to work for Gulf Oil, he lacked only his oral examination and his thesis. Unfortunately, his supervising professor had died, forcing him to change the focus of his thesis. That meant extra course work, additional fieldwork and more time. With the end in sight, his money ran out, and he had to give up his quest again.

Scopes needed a job. But the year was 1932, and the country was in the middle of the Great Depression. He drove back to Paducah to search for a job, later describing himself as "a private in the army of the unemployed." That fall, his first son, John Jr., was born. (A second son, William, would follow a few years later.) It was a joyous occasion, but it added to the urgency of the family's economic situation. One job that Scopes sought was that of politician; he ran for U.S. Congress as a socialist. (Scopes's father also ran as a socialist for public office in 1900 and 1904.) The Great Depression had convinced him that capitalism was on the verge of collapse. James Presley, co-author of Scopes's memoirs, speculates that Scopes ran as a socialist to support the candidacy of Norman Mattoon Thomas, a friend of Scopes's father and six-time presidential candidate for the Socialist Party of America. Not surprisingly, Scopes lost the election.

Scopes finally found a steady job in the summer of 1933 when he went to work as a geologist for the United Production Corporation, later known as the United Gas Corporation. After working in the field for ten months, he was transferred to the general office in Houston. He worked there until 1940, when the offices moved to Shreveport, Louisiana. Scopes worked on various industry-related tasks, such as engineering, appraisals, taxes and regulations. He worked fifty-five to sixty hours a week and often worked on weekends. Luckily, Scopes claimed he needed only about four hours of sleep each night.

In 1960, the movie *Inherit the Wind* came out, and the producer, Stanley Kramer, asked Scopes to help promote the film. He agreed, justifying his participation by saying that "it was time to remind the people again of the importance of preserving their basic freedoms." The movie premiered in Dayton in July, the thirty-fifth anniversary of the trial. Although the film took a few liberties with the facts (Scopes was never arrested and didn't have a girlfriend), Scopes enjoyed the movie. After the premiere, Scopes traveled to Boston, New York, Washington and Los Angeles on what he called the "ballyhoo trail." He also appeared on the television game show *To Tell The Truth*. Scopes was interviewed many times and was often asked if he would do it all over again. Scopes answered: "If I were a young man with no outside obligations, my decision would be the same as it was in 1925."

Scopes retired in 1964 and, looking for something to do with his time, started work on his memoirs. He met his co-author, James Presley, at a party in Shreveport. Presley wrote the entire book except for the preface, which Scopes penned. The book, titled *Center of the Storm*, came out in 1967. Scopes agreed to help promote the book and embarked on a book tour with stops in New York, Massachusetts, Pennsylvania, Texas, California and, of course, Dayton, Tennessee. He also made appearances on many of the major television talk shows, including *The Dick Cavett Show*, *The Mike Douglas Show*, *The Today Show*, *The Merv Griffin Show* and *The Tonight Show Starring Johnny Carson*. He spoke on several college campuses, including his old alma mater, the University of Kentucky. Scopes's last public appearance was at George Peabody College for Teachers (now a part of Vanderbilt University) in Nashville on April 1, 1970.

Sadly, the Scopes family life was not a happy one; Scopes and his wife, Mildred, fought a long battle with alcoholism. Things got so bad that the two boys, John Jr. and Bill, lived away from their parents for three years. During this time, John Jr. was in high school, and Bill was in middle school. The boys lived with Scopes's sister Ethel in Paducah or with his sister Lela

The Rhea County Courthouse in Dayton, Tennessee, where the Scopes trial took place. The building is home to a museum focused on the trial. *Shutterstock*.

in Winnetka. During this time, the boys saw rarely saw their parents. John Jr. claimed that he "couldn't connect" with his father, and both sons described their relationship with their parents as "distant." In fact, John Scopes didn't attend his son Bill's wedding. John Jr. described his father as "a happy drunk" and his mother as "an angry drunk." Bill described his mother as "the meanest bitch I've ever known." According to Bill's wife, Jackie: "When Bill asked me to marry him, he asked only three things of me: Don't yell at me, don't throw things at me, and don't hit me like my mother did. He told me that his mother did things that he couldn't talk about." When the time came for the boys to return to their parents' home in Shreveport, they didn't want to go. John Jr. explained, "We were happy with Ethel and Lela. I didn't want to go back [to Shreveport]." The boys credit their own successful careers not to their parents but to their Aunts Ethel and Lela.

John Scopes died of cancer (he had been a heavy smoker) on October 21, 1970, and is buried in Oak Grove Cemetery in Paducah. The tombstone bears the inscription "A Man of Courage." The Associated Press has ranked the Scopes Monkey Trial as one of the top one hundred events of the twentieth century. The Rhea County Courthouse in Dayton has been designated a National Historic Landmark and houses the Scopes Trial Museum. The courtroom where the drama unfolded is on the second floor. Every summer, in July, the town commemorates the event. It is ironic that Kentucky, the state that gave us John Scopes, is now home to a monument to ignorance called the Creation Museum.

GEORGE DEVOL

1912–2011

Field | Invention
Major Contribution | Invented the world's first industrial robotic arm
Kentucky Connection | Born and raised in Louisville

> *We applied for a patent for this "teachable machine."*
> *Then we thought, why not make a manipulator? If we put*
> *a hand on it, we can move parts around.*
>
> *—Devol in his final interview at age ninety-nine*

GEORGE CHARLES DEVOL JR. was born on February 20, 1912, into an upper-middle-class family living in Louisville. His father was a traffic manager for the Louisville and Nashville Railroad; his mother was a stay-at-home parent. Devol became interested in machines and electricity at an early age. When he was fifteen, he rebuilt the family car's transmission without referring to any instructions. His father recognized Devol's talent and sent him to the Riordan Preparatory Academy in New York. At Riordan, he mingled with "the kind of people you couldn't meet otherwise—sons of diplomats and heads of state, politicians, the very wealthy." The social skills and persuasive powers he learned at the elite school would serve him well in the future when he needed funding for his inventions. The school's freestyle curriculum was also a good fit for Devol. "I wasn't much of a student, and I didn't like sports, but they let me run the electrical power station, and I read everything I could find on engineering and mechanics."

After he graduated from Riordan, Devol's family assumed he would go to college. But Devol had other plans and persuaded his parents to allow him to skip the schooling. "It was a shock for them. I'd been accepted and was all set to go to MIT, but my father finally gave in. He said, 'OK, go ahead and see if you can do it.' And I did do it!" Devol was determined to start his own company.

Of all the new inventions of the time, the one that fascinated Devol the most was "talking pictures." Before the 1930s, movies were silent, with only short subtitles providing narration and dialogue; a piano in the theater provided musical accompaniment. Now "talkies" were taking over. But there was a problem: how to get the sound to synchronize with the images. Devol came up with a solution. "Everybody was excited about 'talkies.' I just approached investors, saying I had a new way of putting sound on film. I got $25,000 here, and $50,000 there, and pretty soon I had enough for my own company. And this was during the Depression! I can't figure out how I did it myself." Devol must have been a persuasive nineteen-year-old.

In 1932, Devol launched a company called United Cinephone with a manufacturing plant in Torrington, Connecticut. Unfortunately, Devol found himself up against some formidable competition. "Being so young, I didn't even think about who I was up against; Western Electric, RCA, AT&T. It was impossible." So Devol dropped the idea and moved on to other things.

Devol had lots of leftover electronic parts and needed an invention that made use of them. "I started thinking about what else we could do with all these photocells and vacuum tubes. I came up with the idea of making photoelectric controls for electric doors." The result was one of the most ubiquitous marvels of the modern world: the automatic door. He licensed the technology to a company called Yale & Towne, which sold it as the "Phantom Doorman"—a photoelectric door that would magically open as a visitor approached.

Devol occasionally missed an opportunity. In 1935, Firestone Tire and Rubber Co. asked Devol to devise a method of sorting packages. The result was an optical barcode system based on photocells; it was an early form of the barcoding system used by retailers today. But Devol thought of it as simply one component of a larger machine and so he never applied for a patent on the device. "Now it's big business, but then, we didn't know what we had. As far as I know, we were using it long before anyone else."

In 1938, Devol went on a blind date with a Hunter College student named Evelyn Jahelka. The couple fell head-over-heels in love and got married on New Year's Eve. George and Evelyn had four children: two sons and two daughters. According to the children, Evelyn was the backbone of the family. She supported George through thick and thin for sixty-five years until her death in 2003.

By the late 1930s, Devol had opened a new and larger manufacturing plant on Long Island. There, he made lighting fixtures, wireless control devices and phonograph amplifiers. In 1939, the company installed automatic photoelectric counters to keep track of the number of visitors to the New York World's Fair. Also on display at the fair was Electro the robot—a big, noisy, theatrical device made by Westinghouse Electric. Electro was just for show; it was not a practical invention. Robots had become a fixture in science fiction tales of the time. Science fiction writer Isaac Asimov coined the word robot in 1941 in a story titled "Liar!" Asimov explained to a friend that he was tired of listing all the activities related to robots, such as design, construction, operations and manufacturing. He wanted one word that would encompass everything, so he invented the word robotics. Contrary to some accounts, Devol was not a fan of science fiction. Fantastic tales of robots did not inspire his future invention.

World War II interrupted Devol's streak of inventions. He sold his interest in United Cinephone because he realized the company wasn't big enough to handle military contracts. "I gave them a very good deal, but I didn't think it all the way through: 'Now what!?'" Devol did his part for the war effort with short stints at several companies. First, he was head of production at Seversky Aircraft on Long Island. It was unchallenging work, and Devol didn't last long. Next, he took some ideas he had about radar technology to Sperry Gyroscope, an electronics company. They hired him as manager of the Special Projects Department, where he was put in charge of developing military radar devices and microwave test equipment. It was during this time that scientists working on radar discovered that microwaves could cook food. Devol was part of a team that developed the first commercial use of microwave oven technology. The result was a vending machine, the "Speedy Weenie," that made its debut in 1947, cooking and dispensing hot dogs.

Later during the war, Devol approached the Auto-Ordnance Company, a firm that manufactured Thompson submachine guns. He convinced the company that radar countermeasures were about to emerge as a defense technology. In 1943, he organized General Electronics Industries (GEI) in Greenwich, Connecticut, as a subsidiary of the Auto-Ordnance Company. Soon, GEI had three thousand employees producing counter-radar devices for the military, some of which flew aboard Allied aircraft on D-Day. When

GEI was offered the biggest military contract in history, Devol objected because he was unsure the company could meet the contract. GEI accepted the contract, and Devol resigned. Finally, Devol joined RCA. But the job was in sales, and Devol complained that it "wasn't his ball of wax." He left RCA after a short time.

As the war wound down, Devol, now a self-employed inventor with a company called Devol Research, began searching for a big idea. He had done some research on a new method of magnetic recording. "Normal magnetic recording has a magnetic pulse, which is read as the tape passes the machine head, but it won't work standing still—something has to move. My idea was the opposite—no continuous tape." So, in 1946, Devol patented a magnetic recording system for controlling machines and a digital playback device.

Now he needed a company to invest in and develop the product. Devol paid a visit to retired general Leslie Groves, the former director of the Manhattan Project, the effort to build an atomic bomb, who was now a vice-president at Remington Rand. Groves offered Devol a development team, and Devol went to work.

At Remington Rand, Devol patented a method of high-speed printing using magnetic tape. It could produce one thousand sheets per minute and was the world's fastest printing press. The company's legal department warned that it should keep the printing press a secret, prompting Devol to joke: "General Groves had two top-secret projects: the atomic bomb and our printer."

Now came Devol's greatest invention. He used the magnetic recording system to create something truly remarkable: a teachable machine. Devol later described how it all worked: "We would hook up the recording system to a machine, a lathe, for example. We turned out whatever parts we wanted, and...magnetically recorded all the lathe's actions." By reversing the process, that is, by playing back the magnetic recording and feeding the information back into the lathe, the lathe could reproduce its actions. "Then we thought, why not make it a manipulator? If we put a hand on it, we can move parts around."

Devol's device would solve a big problem. When a manufacturing company redesigned or replaced a product, the tools used to make the product would also have to be replaced. This resulted in a lot of machine tools in scrap yards. Devol thought this was "wasteful and no way to run a business." His new manipulator eliminated the problem because it could adapt to changes in products. He called this universal automation. Devol's wife, Evelyn, suggested combining the two words into one: Unimation.

In 1954, Devol applied for a patent for a device he called Programmed Article Transfer, a machine that could move and manipulate objects. In his patent application, Devol wrote: "The present invention makes available for the first time a more or less general purpose machine that has universal application to a vast diversity of applications where cyclic digital control is desired." The device became known as the "Unimate." U.S. Patent 2,988,237, which cited no prior inventions, was granted for the Unimate that same year.

Getting a patent was no guarantee of commercial success. Devol needed a company to invest in his device, manufacture it and take it to market. He scoured the country, searching for a company that was willing to take on the invention. Through family connections, Devol finally met his entrepreneurial partner at a cocktail party. His name was Joseph Engelberger, an executive with an engineering degree from Columbia University. Engelberger fell in love with Devol's machine, and the two men made a great team. Engelberger was a charismatic bowtie-wearing extrovert who became the public face of Unimation. Meanwhile, Devol was the introverted inventor who kept the patents rolling in.

At the time, Engelberger was chief of engineering in the aircraft products division at Manning, Maxwell and Moore, located in Stratford, Connecticut. Devol agreed to license his patent to the company. Unfortunately, the company was bought out by Dresser Technologies, and the new owners didn't see a need for the aircraft division or Devol's patent licenses. Luckily, Devol and Engelberger rescued the venture by finding a buyer for the aircraft division. Consolidated Diesel Electronic (Condec) bought the division and agreed to finance the development of Devol's machine. Condec created a division called Unimation Incorporated, with Engelberger as president, to tackle the development of Devol's device.

In 1958, Devol and his six-man crew set up shop in Danbury, Connecticut, and built what would become known as the Unimate. Vacuum tubes controlled the first prototypes but were later replaced by transistors. The "off-the-shelf" parts that were available in the late 1950s were not adequate, so the team designed and engineered nearly every part.

The last step was to market the machine. At first, Engelberger resisted using the word robot to describe the device, thinking it sounded too much like silly science fiction to prospective clients. He preferred to call it a manipulator. But Devol protested and told Engelberger, "If you want to sell something, you have to give it a name people recognize. Nobody knows what a manipulator is. Just call it a robot." Engelberger was persuaded, and they called their creation a robot.

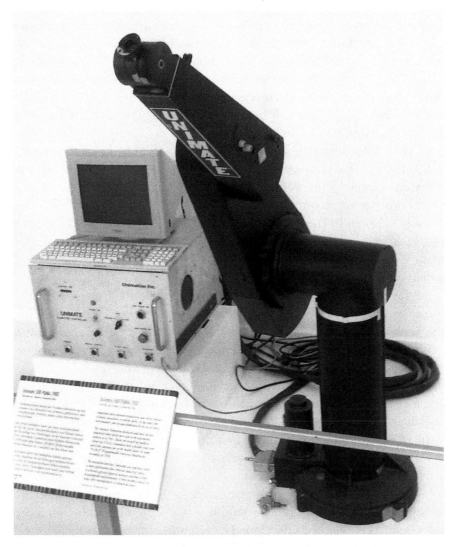

The Unimate 500 Puma robotic arm from 1983 displayed in the Deutsches Museum in Munich, Germany. *Theoprakt/Wikimedia Commons.*

In 1960, Devol sold the first hydraulically powered Unimate robot to General Motors. The next year, GM installed Unimate 001 at its die-casting plant in Trenton, New Jersey. The robot's first task was to pick up hot pieces of metal from a die-casting machine and neatly stack them. Meanwhile, Engelberger and the Unimate were making the rounds on television with appearances on *The Tonight Show with Johnny Carson, The Merv*

Griffith Show and Walter Cronkite's *The Twentieth Century*. As the company expanded into Europe and Japan, Engelberger and the robot could be seen at every expo and trade show. Engelberger's public appearances earned him the title "the father of robotics." But Devol didn't seem to mind, saying Engelberger "deserves a lot of credit. He saw my vision when others didn't. People can call him the 'father,' but I'm the inventor. The patent office says so."

In 1966, GM opened its state-of-the-art plant in Lordstown, Ohio, where 110 cars poured off the assembly line every hour—twice the rate of any other automobile plant. Almost one hundred Unimates aided the plant's prodigious output. Soon after, other automobile makers—Ford, Chrysler, Nissan, Volvo and Fiat—bought Unimates. Then the Unimates expanded into other industries and performed other jobs. The first Unimates simply manipulated materials, but over time, the robots learned how to weld, print and assemble.

At first, the autoworkers union fought against the robots, labeling them "man replacers." Unimation responded to the outcry by retraining the workers to repair and maintain the robots. The jobs the Unimates performed were dirty, dangerous and mind-numbingly dull. And the robots could perform the tasks with precision and without getting tired. Eventually, the unions accepted the existence of the robots. However, modern society is still dealing with the difficulties created by the loss of manufacturing jobs because of automation.

In 1975, Unimation showed its first profit, and in 1978, the company developed the Programmable Universal Machine for Assembly (PUMA), a more versatile robot. Devol continued to generate patents relating to robotics, and Unimation was the first and the biggest robotics company in the world. But then the competition caught up, and the company's sales sank. Manufacturers developed a preference for electrically powered robots rather than Unimation's hydraulically powered machines. Devol and Engelberger saw the writing on the wall and began looking for a buyer for the company. In 1982, Westinghouse bought Unimation for $107 million but kept Engelberger as president. Devol didn't like the deal but reluctantly accepted the inevitable. Unimation was never profitable again. In 1988, Westinghouse sold what was left of the company to Staubli of Switzerland.

After the demise of Unimation, Devol, in his seventies, continued with Devol Research, his own research and consulting company, and was a pioneer in micro-robotics. Over his long career, Devol held thirty-six patents.

An army of robotic arms assembling automobiles. *Shutterstock.*

In 1997, Devol was inducted into the Automation Hall of Fame. Devol's friend Bob Malone recalled that at the ceremony an educational robot rolled up to Devol and exclaimed in a mechanized voice, "Father, so good to see you!" In 2005, *Popular Mechanics* magazine named the Unimate as one of the "Top 50 Inventions of the Past 50 Years." In 2011, Devol was inducted into the National Inventor's Hall of Fame with an induction citation that reads in part: "Devol's patent for the first digitally operated programmable robotic arm represents the foundation of the modern robotics industry." Today, descendants of Devol's Unimate robotic arm can be seen in factories around the world.

Late in his long life, Devol ran a successful business buying and selling boats in Fort Lauderdale, spending winters in Florida and summers in Connecticut. In his nineties, he got hooked on stock market day trading and sat in front of several computer screens watching and analyzing as the markets gyrated. He willingly gave out investment advice and market tips. After his wife died in 2003, he continued to live independently in his own home and drove his own car.

George Devol, who did as much as anyone to usher in the era of robots, died at age ninety-nine on August 11, 2011, from a heart ailment at his home in Wilton, Connecticut. They buried next him to his wife, Evelyn, in Bald Hill Cemetery in Wilton. His four children survive him. He is also survived by his original Unimate robotic arm that sits in the collections of the Smithsonian Institution. The Henry Ford Museum in Dearborn, Michigan, holds another.

JAMES BAKER

1914–2005

Field | Astronomy and optical physics
Major Contribution | Designed telescopes and cameras
Kentucky Connection | Born and raised in Louisville, graduated from
the University of Louisville

> *As a young Harvard astronomer, Dr. James G. Baker designed most of the lenses and many of the cameras used in aerial over-flights of "denied territory" enabling the success of the U.S. peacetime strategic reconnaissance policy.*
>
> *—citation accompanying the Pioneers of National Reconnaissance Medal awarded to Baker in 2000*

We know little about the childhood of **JAMES GILBERT BAKER**, who was born in Louisville on November 11, 1914. Called "Jim" by his friends, he was the fourth child of Jesse B. Baker and Hattie M. Stallard. In 1931, he graduated from Louisville's duPont Manual High School and enrolled at the University of Louisville. He began as a chemistry major but switched to physics and mathematics in 1933 as a result of taking an interdisciplinary science course taught by Walter Lee Moore, an astronomy professor. Baker was an outstanding student, and Moore allowed him to use the department's telescopes. Soon Baker was grinding mirrors and building his own telescopes. He also helped found the Louisville Astronomical Society.

During his college days, Baker met his future wife, Elizabeth Katherine Breitenstein, who was also from the Louisville area. Like Baker, Breitenstein was an excellent student. She was the valedictorian of her high school class and earned a master's degree in mathematics from the University of Wisconsin. The couple married in 1938 and had four children.

Baker graduated from Louisville in 1935 and continued his education at Harvard. At the Harvard College Observatory, Baker collaborated on an important series of scientific papers that focused on the physical processes in gaseous nebulae. He earned his master's degree in astronomy in 1936 and was appointed a Junior Fellow of the prestigious Harvard Society of Fellows, a group of distinguished young scholars just beginning their academic careers. The fellows are allowed to conduct independent research in any field without having to meet formal degree requirements or receiving grades. In 1940, Baker designed what became known as the Baker-Schmidt telescope. The telescope was actually a camera that eliminated astigmatism and an effect known as a coma in which stars appeared to have a tail like a comet. In 1941, just before the United States entered World War II, Baker was awarded a small contract by the army to develop a wide-angle reconnaissance camera. This minor task subsequently led to over one hundred other projects.

Baker was awarded his doctorate in astronomy in a rather unusual way. According to the *Courier-Journal Magazine*, during an astronomy department dinner in 1942, the director of the Harvard observatory, Harlow Shapley, asked Baker to give an impromptu talk. It must have been a great talk, because immediately afterward, "Dr. Shapley stood up and proclaimed an on-the-spot departmental meeting and asked for a vote on recommending Baker for a Ph.D. based on the 'oral exam' he had just finished. The vote was unanimous." And so it was that Jim became "Dr. Baker."

Baker was named director of the Observatory Optical Project at Harvard and from 1943 through 1945 spent countless hours performing calculations that allowed him to design aerial cameras. This was, of course, before electronic calculators, so Baker did his calculations using a Marchant mechanical calculator. After designing a camera and building a prototype, the instrument needed to be tested. Baker risked his life by flying in airplanes sitting in an unpressurized compartment so that he could test his equipment. During this time, he also began a long association with the PerkinElmer Corporation as an optical consultant. Recognition for Baker's wartime work came in 1948 when he received the Presidential Medal of Merit.

After World War II, Baker became a professor and research associate at Harvard and was the first to use computers to make optical calculations.

The SR-71 "Blackbird" strategic reconnaissance aircraft carried Baker-Nunn cameras onboard to take photographs. *USAF/Judson Brohmer/Wikimedia Commons.*

Using the Harvard Mark II, a giant electromechanical computer completed in 1947, Baker ran an optical ray-tracing program. As computer technology progressed in the 1960s and 1970s, Baker's own children wrote computer programs to assist with his complex calculations. In 1948, he moved to California for a two-year stint as a research associate at the Lick Observatory. He returned to Harvard in 1950.

During the Cold War era of the 1950s, Baker worked on cameras for the famous U-2 spy plane. At the time, the Soviet Union would not allow U.S. planes to fly in its airspace. But we needed a way to watch what the Russians were up to. The solution was to use aircraft flying at a high altitude of seventy thousand feet. This put the aircraft beyond the range of Soviet MIG aircraft, which could only fly up to an altitude of about forty-five thousand feet, and beyond the reach of Soviet radar, which could not track aircraft flying above sixty-five thousand feet. Such an aircraft would require cameras that could take panoramic high-resolution aerial photographs. Baker designed the cameras that photographed Soviet troops and missiles. Intelligence obtained from the U-2 spying missions eased concerns about Soviet military superiority during the Eisenhower administration. By 1958, Baker was almost solely responsible for all the cameras used by photoreconnaissance aircraft. During the 1960s, similar cameras were used to identify launching sites during the Cuban Missile Crisis. Baker also helped design the camera systems for the SR-71 Blackbird, in use from the mid-1960s to the 1990s.

During the late 1950s, scientists and military leaders anticipated the launching of the first satellites into space. Baker collaborated with engineer Joseph Nunn to build the Baker-Nunn satellite tracking camera. Baker was responsible for the camera; Nunn built the mechanical tracking systems. The camera had a wide field of view so it could photograph large swaths of sky and track the paths of spacecraft and other objects. When the Soviets launched Sputnik in October 1957, a dozen Baker-Nunn cameras were in position around the world to watch it. For the next thirty years, the Baker-Nunn cameras were used to determine the exact orbits of spacecraft.

In 1966, Edwin Land, the co-founder of the Polaroid Corporation, convinced Baker to become a consultant to the company. Land wanted Baker to design the optics for a new camera that would almost instantly produce

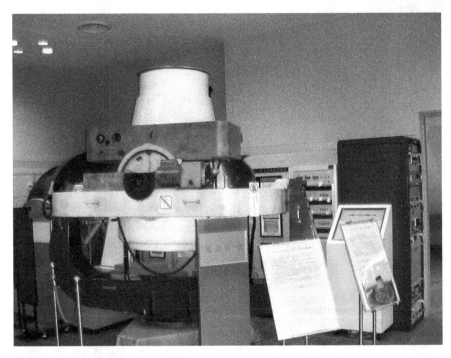

A Baker-Nunn camera used for satellite tracking in the 1960s. *Wikimedia Commons.*

a color photograph without the user having to apply messy chemicals. The revolutionary SX-70 Land camera with optics by Baker debuted on the national market in 1973 and was an immediate success, selling over 700,000 units by the middle of 1974. Even famous professional photographers, including Andy Warhol and Ansel Adams, used the camera. Although digital photography made the camera obsolete, it still has a cult following today. For the next thirty-five years, Baker designed products for Polaroid. Most notable among these was his design of the focusing system for the 1986 Polaroid Spectra camera.

Baker continued his affiliation with the Harvard-Smithsonian Center for Astrophysics until his retirement in 2003. In his basement workshop, he continued to work on a new telescope design he told his family he should have invented in 1940. He never finished his last project. Baker died at his home in Bedford, New Hampshire, on June 29, 2005. He was ninety years old. Over his long and remarkable career, Baker published over thirty papers and held over fifty U.S. patents. In 1945, he wrote a book with George Dimitroff titled *Telescopes and Accessories*. Interestingly, Baker's four children followed their father's footsteps into scientific and technical careers.

Baker was elected as a member of the National Academy of Sciences in 1979. In a memorial tribute, Baker was remembered as "a friend, a gentleman, a scholar, a patriot of the highest integrity, and a truly inspirational engineer of uniquely difficult accomplishments."

WILLIAM LIPSCOMB

1919-2011

Field | Chemistry
Major Accomplishment | Won the Nobel Prize for chemistry in 1976
  for work on the structure of molecules and chemical bonding
Kentucky Connection | Raised in Lexington, graduated from the
  University of Kentucky

> *I also think there's a lack of general education in people
> who are not taking science, who don't study science, who
> major say in humanities or social science in their schools.
> This means that the political decisions are made by
> people who do not have a background in science, which
> I think is a sorta sad thing.*

> *—Lipscomb in an interview on YouTube*

WILLIAM NUNN LIPSCOMB JR. was born in Cleveland, Ohio, on December 9, 1919, to William and Edna Lipscomb. Within a year, the family moved to Lexington, where Lipscomb grew up with sisters Virginia and Helen. Lipscomb's father was a doctor, a general practitioner who made house calls. His mother was a music teacher. In an autobiographical sketch, Lipscomb explained that because of his parent's busy work schedules, his early home environment encouraged independence, personal responsibility and self-reliance—personal qualities that would stay with Lipscomb throughout his life.

The family lived at 132 Rosemont Garden in Lexington (the house still stands). The house, at about 1,350 square feet, is small by today's standards and sits on a quarter-acre lot. A front porch runs along the front of the house with the overhang supported by four columns. According to current real estate information, the house has three bedrooms and one bathroom.

There must have been something in the neighborhood's drinking water because within one hundred yards of his house, five other boys in Lipscomb's age group eventually entered science-related fields: two boys became physicists, another two physicians and one an engineer. Lipscomb fondly recalled their scientific adventures: "Morse-coded messages over a wire stretched high across the street, crystal sets, Tom Swift [the boy Edison-like inventor] books, electric arcs, and lots of talk about astronomy and then chemistry occupied us in a far more interesting way than did the school work."

They taught very little science at Lipscomb's elementary school, but he studied independently and collected rock, insect and animal specimens. He developed a particular interest in astronomy and attended public viewing nights at the University of Kentucky's observatory. There, he became a lifelong friend of Professor H.H. Dowing, who gave Lipscomb a book on astronomy he read and reread. The book remains in the family's possession, and on page 432, Lipscomb underlined a sentence: "The stars are too hot to burn." This statement puzzled Lipscomb (as it would anyone) because the stars were so bright. The answer to the question of what makes the stars shine wouldn't be answered until 1938, when Hans Bethe explained it using nuclear fusion. On the inside of the back cover, young Lipscomb wrote some notes, including the word molecule followed by atom, then proton accompanied by a plus sign and "eletron [*sic*]."

Lipscomb's father served as a physician at a Boy Scout summer camp for several summers and took young William with him. Lipscomb worked his way up the scouting ranks to a Star Scout, two ranks below Eagle Scout. Later, the family spent two summers in a log cabin on the shore of Deer Lake in Minnesota. While camping out in the open in a sleeping bag, Lipscomb remembered watching a meteor shower where the streaks of light in the night sky were so numerous and bright that they woke him up.

When Lipscomb was eleven, he got a chemistry set for Christmas. Instead of experimenting with it for a while and then abandoning it as most kids are wont to do, Lipscomb stuck with it. He ordered chemicals and pieces of apparatus from suppliers and also used his father's account at the local drugstore to buy chemicals at a discount. This was during the Great Depression. He entertained visitors with chemical demonstrations involving color changes, odors and explosions. His mother later recalled that "he'd made stuff that smells so bad—rotten-egg gas—to chase the girls out. You couldn't go into the house for hours." She tolerated Lipscomb's chemical experiments and only objected once, when he tried to isolate urea from his own urine. Lipscomb's home chemistry lab grew and grew. When he graduated, he donated it to his high school, more than doubling the school's inventory of equipment.

By the time Lipscomb took his first chemistry class at Picadome (now Lafayette) High School, he knew as much as, if not more than, his teacher, L. Frederic Jones. Realizing he had a scientific prodigy, Jones gave Lipscomb his college chemistry textbooks and simply asked him to take the final exam. Lipscomb spent most of his time in the back of the chemistry room, where he was engaged in his own chemical research. By the end of the year, Lipscomb, a sophomore, was actually teaching qualitative analysis to the class of seniors. Surprisingly, Lipscomb earned a C in the class. Why? Because the final exam required memorizing the first ten elements on the periodic table, and Lipscomb wouldn't do it. Lipscomb reasoned, "I could just look it up. So I didn't do it."

The next year, Lipscomb took physics and won first prize in a statewide competition in the subject. He continued to read on his own and was especially influenced by the book *Flatland* by Edwin Abbott. This famous book, first published in 1884, is a mathematical fantasy that explores the multiple dimensions of space. The book piqued Lipscomb's interest in Einstein's theory of relativity. He also read the philosophical book *Man, the Unknown* by Alexis Carrel multiple times.

Lipscomb's sister Helen contracted polio in 1937 at age seventeen, an illness that had a profound effect on the family. Because patients did not want to come into physical contact with a physician who had a family member with polio, Lipscomb's father had to close his medical practice and switch fields to psychiatry, working from a home office. Helen couldn't go to school, so Lipscomb tutored her in mathematics and other subjects.

Lipscomb went to college at the University of Kentucky (UK) on a music scholarship and played in the marching band. A summer job selling seeds to farmers helped pay tuition, and he could live at home and avoid room and board. He confessed to having "no desire to become the fourth generation of physicians in the family" and instead seriously considered a career in music.

But his college coursework steered Lipscomb toward science. In physics, he took classes in thermodynamics, quantum mechanics and electricity and magnetism. In chemistry, a course in qualitative organic analysis was influential. After Lipscomb completed the class, his professor suggested he undertake a research problem. He agreed, and the work resulted in Lipscomb's first scientific publication.

But it was mathematics that appears to have ultimately swayed Lipscomb toward a career in science. Someone later asked Lipscomb why he became a chemist instead of a musician. His answer? "A math class. A math class taught by a German named Fritz John." Lipscomb was the only student in the class taught one summer by John. The subject was vector analysis, and it introduced Lipscomb to matrices and tensors. The pair also played with Maxwell's equations from physics, four equations that govern all of electricity and magnetism.

Besides his formal coursework, Lipscomb continued his program of independent study by reading books on atomic physics and quantum mechanics. In particular, Lipscomb recalled reading a famous scientific book titled *The Nature of the Chemical Bond* by Linus Pauling. Pauling, a professor at Caltech, was arguably the greatest chemist of the twentieth century and would eventually win two Nobel Prizes, one for chemistry and the other for peace. As we shall see, Pauling would play a pivotal role in Lipscomb's career.

Lipscomb graduated from UK in 1941 with a degree in chemistry. His next big decision was which graduate school to attend. He applied to Columbia but received a polite rejection letter from chemist and Nobel laureate Harold Urey. Northwestern offered a research assistantship worth $150 per month. The chair of UK's chemistry department favored a fellowship at MIT. And Caltech offered a teaching assistantship in physics for $200 per month. Lipscomb chose Caltech "primarily because of the need for a stimulating environment, and for research problems that were more current." So, in the late summer, Lipscomb hitchhiked all the way from Lexington to Pasadena. During the journey, Lipscomb's mother remembered receiving a postcard with "Thumb Fun" printed on the back.

Lipscomb started out in the physics department and took a class in particle physics from Robert Oppenheimer, head of the Manhattan Project and the "father" of the atomic bomb. But after a semester, he came under the spell of Linus Pauling, "to whom I was drawn by his penetrating and imaginative comments at colloquia." He switched to the chemistry department just as World War II began. Although Lipscomb did not serve in the active military, he, along with other graduate students, did work on war-related research projects as part of the National Defense

Research Council program at Caltech. Lipscomb's war research included a study of how to obscure Los Angeles using smoke particles to prevent an aerial attack. He also worked on nitroglycerin-nitrocellulose propellants that required him to handle pure nitroglycerin, no doubt a rather nerve-wracking endeavor. How does one carry a beaker of nitroglycerin? Lipscomb later explained to his son that the safest way to carry the vials was by the fingertips, so the heat of your hand did not detonate the liquid, and your knuckles pointed outward to absorb the shock. Not wearing gloves reduced the chances of dropping the dangerous solution. Lipscomb incorporated his war work into his doctoral thesis. As a result, two chapters of his thesis had to be classified.

Lipscomb's thesis research focused on deducing the structure of molecules by shooting beams of electrons or X-rays at a sample, a method called electron or X-ray diffraction. Most significantly, Lipscomb and a colleague used X-ray diffraction to measure the distance of a chemical single bond between carbon and nitrogen, a measurement that Pauling needed for his work with a group of chemicals known as peptides, which are short strings of amino acids.

Along the way, Lipscomb had some notable experiences, both good and bad. One story from his early years that Lipscomb enjoyed telling was about making an unassisted triple play during a baseball game with the Caltech chemistry department team. Lipscomb told the story like this: "With the bases loaded and nobody out I was playing center field…and a guy hit a line drive over second base, and I came charging in and got it at the shoe-tops, that's out one, and I stepped on second base, that's out two [getting the runner from second who did not get back to the base to tag up after the catch], and tagged the guy that came in from first base.…I didn't realize I had three outs. I threw it to third base and we got the fourth out. But it was an unassisted triple play, and it made the Pasadena newspapers."

One tragic incident occurred in September 1943. Elizabeth Swingle, the chemistry stockroom keeper, was carrying a bottle of a chemical called ethyl chloroformate when it exploded in her hands. She was standing in the elevator, and Lipscomb was down the hall. Lipscomb ran to her and pulled her under a shower. But he was too late. She had inhaled too much of the noxious chemical, which forms hydrochloric acid in the lungs. She suffered major tissue damage and died eight hours later. The accident prompted Linus Pauling to write to the chemical's supplier, Eastman Kodak, to demand a review of its safety procedures. Caltech reviewed its own safety equipment and precautions and made necessary changes. Evidently, the experience stayed with Lipscomb for the rest of his life. A colleague remembered Lipscomb being obsessed with safety equipment in the late 1970s.

It was during his time at Caltech that Lipscomb met his first wife, Mary Adele Sargent, who was working as a lab assistant in the chemistry department. (Her name would be shortened to "Marydell.") The couple married on May 20, 1944, at Immaculate Conception Catholic Church in Monrovia, California. The marriage would last nearly forty years, and they would have three children. The first child, an unnamed son, died a few hours after birth. The two surviving children were a daughter, Dorothy, and a son, James.

Lipscomb learned some valuable scientific lessons from his thesis advisor, Linus Pauling, especially about choosing research problems. In 1991, Lipscomb recalled: "When I was growing up and learning science and all through my undergraduate days, I thought the worst thing you could possibly do is publish something that is wrong. It turns out that's not right. Linus taught me that. It is much worse to work on something that is dull." And in 1995, he stated, "It is much better to risk an occasional error in interesting and original research than to be always right in less original or more prosaic studies." Nevertheless, Lipscomb was profoundly distressed on those very rare occasions when he was wrong.

Lipscomb finished his doctorate in the summer of 1946 and accepted a position as an assistant professor of physical chemistry at the University of Minnesota. His productivity as a researcher resulted in a rapid ascent up the academic career ladder. He was promoted to associate professor in 1950 and was named a full professor in 1954.

Lipscomb's son, James, remembered two rules in the early Lipscomb household. The first was: "Don't wake daddy." If Lipscomb didn't get a good night's sleep, he couldn't work on anything difficult the next day. Lipscomb expounded on this rule: "For me, the creative process, first of all, requires a good nine hours of sleep a night. Second, it must not be pushed by the need to produce practical applications." The second rule was about butter. As your knife traveled the short distance from the butter dish to the dinner roll, it was permissible for others to swoop in with their own knives and steal a dab of butter. This came as a shock to the occasional dinner guest.

During his Minnesota years, Lipscomb's research focused on the crystalline structure of boranes, a group of chemical compounds made from the elements boron and hydrogen that are highly reactive when in contact with other chemicals. The experimental science of determining the arrangement and bonding of atoms in a crystal is called crystallography. But to study the boranes, the crystallography had to be performed at low temperatures. One problem for this type of work was condensation, which, at least during the Minnesota winters, the group minimized by simply opening the windows to let in the frigid, dry air. Other problems were not so easy to solve and presented difficult technological challenges for Lipscomb and his research group. They overcame the obstacles and developed innovative technology that allowed the use of X-ray diffraction on a single borane crystal at low temperatures. The research culminated in a 1954 paper titled "The Valence Structures of the Boron Hydrides." According to a biography by Douglas Rees, one of Lipscomb's students, "This paper opened a new era in the understanding of the chemical bond, and it was at the heart of Lipscomb's Nobel Prize citation."

It was at Minnesota that students started calling Lipscomb "the Colonel" in recognition of his Kentucky roots. The nickname was started by Lipscomb's first graduate student, Murray King, although at first, the label was not used in Lipscomb's presence. The name stuck, Lipscomb liked it and he began telling students to "call me the Colonel." It wasn't until 1973 that Lipscomb received an official "Kentucky Colonel" award from Governor Wendell Ford. According to Lipscomb's son, of all the awards that Lipscomb won, it was the only one that hung in his bedroom. It was perhaps at this point in his life that Lipscomb started wearing string ties like those that adorn the neck of Colonel Sanders of Kentucky Fried Chicken fame. In fact, there is a short YouTube video in which an elderly Lipscomb shows how to tie a string tie.

In 1959, Lipscomb was offered a position at Harvard University, and while he was happy at Minnesota, it was an offer he couldn't refuse. The Harvard chemistry department was one of the best in the country and had brilliant graduate students. On the top floor of the Gibbs Laboratory at Harvard, the desks of graduate students were packed close together, encouraging collaborations between theorists and experimentalists. Lipscomb would remain at Harvard until he officially retired in 1990.

At Harvard, Lipscomb pursued more complex problems in chemical bonding and structure, now aided by a new tool: the computer. His research group calculated molecular orbitals and determined the structure of digestive enzymes. He also did pioneering work using nuclear magnetic resonance to study chemical shifts, a phenomenon that can help uncover the structure of a molecule.

Over time, the group focused more of its efforts on determining the structure of protein molecules using crystallography. One protein was carboxypeptidase A (CPA), a chemical produced in the pancreas and

Left: William Lipscomb won the Nobel Prize for chemistry in 1976. Notice the string tie he was famous for wearing. *James S. Lipscomb/Wikimedia Commons.*

Below: The campus of Harvard University in Cambridge, Massachusetts. *Shutterstock.*

important in many processes in the human body, including digestion, blood clotting and reproduction. The structure of CPA was solved in 1967. They then turned their attention to an enzyme called aspartate carbamoyltransferase (ACTase), a chemical important in the formation of nucleic acids. The group solved the structure of this molecule in the early 1970s.

As Rees tells the story, early on the morning of October 18, 1976, he and a friend were in the student room next to Lipscomb's office when they overheard a phone call picked up by a student. After they heard the words "Nobel Prize" during the conversation, they called the *Boston Globe* to find out who had won. The answer was: Professor Lipscomb of Harvard University. Rees and his buddy ran to Lipscomb's office to deliver the news: "Congratulations, you've won the Nobel Prize." Lipscomb responded, "Are you sure?"

The students were correct, Lipscomb had won the coveted prize all by himself; he didn't share the prize with anyone else. (Today, most of the Nobel Prizes awarded in the sciences are shared between two or three scientists.) The Nobel Prize citation reads, "For his studies on the structure of boranes illuminating problems of chemical bonding." Lipscomb's research helped scientists understand how atoms bind together within molecules. Was the chemistry of boranes sufficient for a Nobel Prize? Lipscomb's son speculated that his father really won for three contributions to chemistry: boron chemistry, large molecule crystallography and nuclear magnetic resonance. The problem is that the rules for the Nobel Prize stipulate that the award must be given for a single achievement, so the citation specified the chemistry of boranes. Lipscomb's son claims his father reached the same conclusion.

Many factors contributed to Lipscomb's success as a scientist, but one ingredient was his work ethic. Lipscomb's son recalls his father worked twelve hours a day, six days a week, plus nine hours on Sunday, for a total of over eighty hours a week. Lipscomb's only vacation came during the summer, when he attended a music camp. As a result, the house was a quiet place, and the children became independent and resourceful. But work wasn't really "work" for Lipscomb, it was play.

Lipscomb was also an excellent teacher and saw the two activities as complementary. "When I do research, I get materials for my lectures, and when I teach I get ideas for my research." Rees asserted that Lipscomb was comfortable teaching anything from general chemistry to advanced graduate courses and that his lectures were "models of clarity." Over the course of his career, Lipscomb taught thirteen different chemistry courses and once told

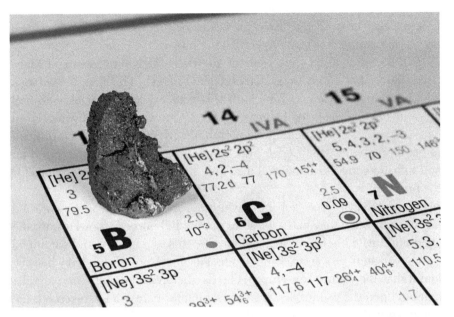

Lipscomb's Nobel Prize was awarded for his work on boranes—chemicals in which the element boron is bonded to hydrogen atoms. *Shutterstock.*

Lipscomb studied the structure of large molecules by shooting beams of X-rays at crystals and examining the diffraction pattern. The technique is called crystallography. *Shutterstock.*

his son that if he needed to learn a new area of chemistry, the first thing he'd do was to volunteer to teach a class on the subject.

In 1983, after thirty-nine years of marriage, Lipscomb divorced Mary Adele and, that same year, married Jean Evans. The couple had one adopted daughter, Jenna. Lipscomb was very private about his personal life and never discussed the reasons for his divorce with anyone. From outward appearances, neither Lipscomb nor Mary Adele seemed difficult to get along with. Mary Adele was known as an outgoing person and an enthusiastic conversationalist. Thus, only the couple knew the reasons for the breakup.

Lipscomb had a wonderful and playful sense of humor. His son remembered an occasion when they had a guest for dinner. Bill pushed a bowl toward the guest and invited her to have a walnut. She took the top nut and continued the conversation as she cracked it open. The guest looked puzzled when she found that the walnut was empty. The day before, Lipscomb had carefully cracked open the walnut, leaving the two hemispheres intact, taken out the nut and glued the shell back together.

On another occasion, Lipscomb was having trouble with the wall clock outside his Harvard office. The problem was that the clock ran five minutes slow, which resulted in Lipscomb being five minutes late to lectures. He called to have it fixed, but the building and grounds people informed him that all the clocks on campus were linked by a central control and that if they adjusted his clock, all the other clocks would be wrong. Frustrated, Lipscomb took the clock off the wall, removed the cover, placed the minute-hand in a vise, and bent it until the tip pointed to the correct time.

Lipscomb once said: "Humor, in my opinion, is an essential part of presentation in science." He put that philosophy into practice in his scientific papers. A note for a 1967 paper reads: "We wish to thank the Office of Navel Research." The "Navel," meaning a bellybutton, should have been "Naval." Lipscomb caught the mistake but left it in the paper as a joke. A 1968 paper contains the following acknowledgement: "We also thank Alice, the cow, who while nevertheless still living, supplied the pancreatic juice from which our crystals of the enzyme carboxypeptidase were obtained." A 1971 paper thanks "Al Powder for assistance in the calibration of the unit cell parameters." One of the samples in the experiment had been labeled "Al powder" since "Al" is the chemical symbol for aluminum. But someone in the research group thought it was the name of a person. And a 1972 paper contains this line: "We admittedly made this observation with the benefit of hindsight. This science is known as retrospectroscopy."

From 1993 until 2010, Lipscomb was an enthusiastic presenter and participant in the Ig Noble Prizes, a satiric, tongue-in-cheek award celebrating trivial or unusual scientific achievements that make people first laugh, then think. He was the prized catch in the very first "Win-a-Date-with-a-Nobel Laureate" in 1993. He danced in the first and only performance of the ballet *The Interpretive Dance of the Electrons*, and he sang in scientific operas like *The Jargon Opera* and *The Count of Infinity*.

Influenced by his musical mother, he played the clarinet from an early age and continued to play throughout his adult life. He performed in chamber groups and was the principal clarinetist with the Pasadena and Minneapolis Civic Orchestras. In 1980, Lipscomb played with a string quartet in the German town of Lindau and garnered this positive review, translated from German: "The slim American Nobel Prize winner...was as relaxed as can be as he played Mozart's Clarinet Quintet....He filled the role exactly that Mozart had assigned to the clarinet not as a solo part, but an inner partnership, an integrated clarinet-string combination. Striking was the beautiful tone formation...the evenness of the rise and fall of the musical phrases, and the extended breath control, as if this were the easiest thing in the world!"

In a 2001 interview, Lipscomb was asked about the important role music had played in his life. He explained that music was a diversion because when he was playing the clarinet, he couldn't think about chemistry. He explained that music is a creative art "because the notes have to be phrased properly and the structure of the piece you have to imagine yourself and sometimes it's different from what the composer meant, but you are creating things there and it's the same kind of creative process that we use in science. The scientific method, as people usually think of it, is not such an orderly process."

William Lipscomb, one of the greatest chemists of the twentieth century, died on April 14, 2011, at age ninety-one. His body was cremated. He rebelled against the idea of retirement, saying that it was tantamount to "giving up." They forced him to retire at age seventy, the mandatory retirement age at Harvard, but he continued to work and do research until the end of his life. His son claimed he was working all day every day at age eighty-seven. Lipscomb once rhetorically asked a student: "What's the point of doing this if you aren't going to publish?" And he practiced what he preached. Over his career, Lipscomb published an astonishing 667 scientific papers, the last of which was published in 2012, the year after he died. Two of his doctoral students, Roald Hoffman and Thomas Steitz, won the Nobel Prize for Chemistry.

WILLIAM ENGLISH

1929–2020

Field | Electrical Engineering
Major Contribution | Co-inventor of the computer mouse
Kentucky Connection | Born and raised in Lexington, graduated from the University of Kentucky

> *Well, I could see it. I could see people reacting to it, but that's tempered by the fact that I'm really concentrating on making it work and coordinating the roles of various people.*
>
> *—Bill English in a 2013 YouTube video responding to the question "Did you have a sense of the impact it [The Mother of All Demos] was having on the audience?"*

WILLIAM KIRK ENGLISH (called "Bill" by his friends) was born in Lexington on January 27, 1929, the year that saw the onset of the Great Depression. His father, Harry English, was an electrical engineer who managed coal mines in eastern Kentucky and West Virginia. His mother, Caroline (Gray) English, was a homemaker. He had two half brothers from his father's previous marriage. After attending elementary school in Lexington, English enrolled in a boarding school near Tucson, Arizona. Upon graduation, he returned to Lexington and followed in his father's footsteps by studying electrical engineering at the University of Kentucky.

English then joined the navy and served as an officer in Japan and at Port Hueneme in California. After the navy, he earned a master's degree in electrical engineering at the University of New Mexico; worked on a bomb scope for military aircraft at Sandia National Laboratory in Albuquerque; and did research at the University of Chicago, Berkeley and Stanford. In the early 1960s, English landed a job at the Stanford Research Institute (now called SRI International), a nonprofit research lab in Menlo Park, California, near the campus of Stanford University. His first assignment was to work on magnetic logic technology.

William "Bill" English, co-inventor of the computer mouse. *Marcin Wichary/Wikimedia Commons.*

In 1964, he was the first person to join Douglas Engelbart's lab. Engelbart was a visionary and an important figure in the history of computing. Back then, the only people using computers were experts who used the machines for complex mathematical calculations, such as solving differential equations. But Engelbart recognized the enormous potential for computers. In 1951, Engelbart had a sudden epiphany, which he described in an interview with *Wired* magazine:

> *All of a sudden—wham!—I got an image of myself sitting at a big CRT [cathode ray tube] screen with all kinds of symbols on it, new and different ones, manipulated by a computer that could be operated through various input devices. All the material on the screen could be controlled with great flexibility. Other people had their display units tied to the same computer complex, and you could connect them. Everybody could share knowledge. The vision unfolded rapidly, in about a half hour, and suddenly the potential of interactive, collaborative computing became totally clear.*

With English as his chief engineer, Engelbart began developing interactive hardware and software that allowed computer users to manipulate text and images on the screen. One important step in this process was coming up with a device that could move a cursor around on the screen to select text and images. Engelbart came up with an idea, wrote some brief notes and made a sketch. He handed the scribbles to English, who was tasked with creating it. "We were working on text

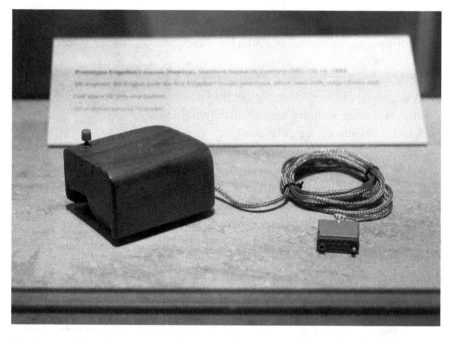

The first prototype computer mouse designed by Douglas Engelbart and built by Bill English. *Michael Hicks/Wikimedia Commons.*

editing—the goal was a device that would be able to select characters and words," English explained to the Computer History Museum in 1999. The device became known as a "mouse."

The first computer mouse, built by English in 1964, was a palm-sized wooden box with a button on top and two wheels positioned at right angles on the bottom. The wheels translated the motion of the mouse into cursor movement on the screen. English was also the very first person to use a computer mouse. In 1972, English took the device a step further by replacing the wheels with a ball that could monitor movement in any direction. This became known as the "ball mouse" and was standard equipment on all personal computers until the optical mouse became available in 1998. In the patent application, filed in 1967, the device was called the "X-Y Position Indicator for a Display System." A patent was awarded in 1970, and SRI licensed the technology to Apple, Xerox and other companies. The device became available in 1984. Neither Engelbart nor English got rich from the invention because the patent was owned by their employer, SRI. The institute profited about $40,000 ($130,000 in today's dollars) when it licensed the device to Apple.

Why was it called a "mouse"? The origin of the name is a mystery—of the five or six people involved in the mouse's development, no one can remember. They had to call it something, and according to English, "brown box with buttons didn't work." But faulty memories aside, there must have been a reason for calling it a mouse—they didn't just pull the name out of thin air. The most likely explanation comes from the fact that they initially had a wire coming out of the box like a little tail. Also, the cursor was called a "CAT."

The mouse had competition from other devices. Light pens, joysticks and tracking balls were also used for the same purpose. In 1966, Engelbart and English asked NASA to fund a study to determine which was the best device for controlling a cursor. NASA was interested in pointing devices because it could use them in a space capsule so that astronauts could interact with computers. "We set up our experiments and the mouse won in every category, even though it had never been used by the test subjects," Engelbart later recalled. "It was faster, and with it people made fewer mistakes."

The mouse made its first public appearance at the Fall Joint Computer Conference in San Francisco on December 9, 1968. Engelbart was the speaker, but English choreographed the entire presentation from the back of the auditorium. In the mid-1950s, English had volunteered as a stage manager for an area theater group called the Actor's Workshop. Now he applied his theatrical talents to show off the computer. He used a projector the size of a Volkswagen Beetle, borrowed from a nearby NASA facility, to show video images of Engelbart as he did his demos. And he could set up the wireless link that sent video from the Menlo Park lab to the auditorium by befriending a telephone company technician. English's efforts paid off; the entire presentation happened without a hitch.

Engelbart began the presentation by asking a provocative question: "If, in your office, you, as an intellectual worker, were supplied with a computer display backed up by a computer that was alive for you all day, and was instantly responsive to every action you have—how much value could you derive from that?" His first demonstration was word processing. He typed "word word word word" on the screen. "If I make some mistakes, I can back up a little bit," Engelbart explained as he showed the delete function. He also showed how blocks of text could be copied and pasted and how items could be reordered by dragging and dropping. Next, he showed off the computer's graphical user interface, which had been created largely by English. He pulled up a map of his route home from work showing planned stops at the grocery store, drugstore and library. "Library. What am I supposed to do

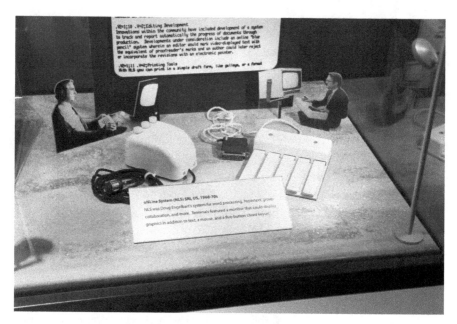

Components of Douglas Engelbart's oNLine System (NLS). Shown here are a three-button mouse and a five-chord keyboard. *Michael Hicks/Wikimedia Commons.*

there?" he asked. A click on the word "Library" pulled up a list. "Oh, I see. Overdue books." This was a hypertext link. Then came a demonstration of video conferencing by linking up with an associate to demonstrate the mouse. Another conference, this time with a colleague in Menlo Park, showed how they could collaboratively edit the same document. Finally, Engelbart showed how SRI would become the second point of a new communications network called the ARPANet, a precursor to the internet.

When Engelbart finished, one thousand computer engineers stood up and cheered. It was one of the most pivotal moments in the history of computing and has become known as "The Mother of All Demos." (Videos of the famous demonstration can be seen on YouTube.) It was a preview of the potential power of computers, but another fifteen years would pass before Apple commercialized the mouse and the graphical user interface. And it would be forty years before Google docs, sheets and slides popularized document sharing.

In the mid-1960s, English and Engelbart were recruited to take part in a research project at the International Foundation for Advanced Study, a private research institute in Menlo Park. The project's aim was to test the effect of the hallucinogenic drug lysergic acid diethylamide, better known as LSD, on human creativity. About 350 test subjects, including many engineers, were given controlled doses of the drug and asked to complete questionnaires about whether the drug had helped their mental processes, given them a better understanding of art and beauty or resulted in a religious experience. English never talked much about his experiences, but Engelbart continued to be an advocate for the project. The research came to an abrupt halt in 1966 when California outlawed the use of LSD. Two years later, the federal government also made the drug illegal. Although the LSD research stopped, use of the drug continued. Apple co-founder Steve Jobs used the drug to enhance his creativity. Some have even kiddingly suggested that the PC wouldn't have been invented without LSD. Today, many in Silicon Valley's computer industry take microdoses of LSD to enhance their performance in a competitive environment.

Although Engelbart's 1968 demonstration had been a success, his lab members were growing frustrated by his complete lack of interest in commercializing the lab's innovations. In 1970, the Xerox Corporation established PARC (the Palo Alto Research Center) with the goal of creating the office of the future. PARC began assembling a team of scientists and engineers to work toward this goal and raided the SRI lab for talent. English, enticed by the opportunity to head his own lab and work toward commercialization, was the first member of Engelbart's team to make the jump. English became a mentor for the younger members of PARC, especially Alan Kay, who shared Engelbart's vision of what computers might someday do. Kay's problem was that he came from the academic world, where research grants were easy to get. But the bureaucrats at PARC were skeptical of Kay's vision of computers simple enough for a child to use and were reluctant to release the purse strings. English tutored Kay about planning and budgets. "I'm afraid I really did ask Bill, 'What's a budget?'" Kay later admitted. English helped Kay draft a plan for a device that would display text and graphics on a display screen. The result was $230,000 to fund the project. Over time, the idea morphed into the Xerox Alto workstation, the world's first personal computer.

English worked for Sun Microsystems in 1989, where he was director of internationalization. Later, he joined the pioneering electronic game console maker 3DO. After retirement, English occasionally consulted on patent issues related to the mouse and early computing systems.

English kept his personal life private. We know that his first marriage, to Patricia Dickson, ended in divorce. He met his second wife, Roberta Mercer, at SRI, where she was Engelbart's secretary. He had two sons,

Aaron and John, from his first marriage, and a stepdaughter, Patricia, from the second.

At a 2008 celebration commemorating the fortieth anniversary of "The Mother of All Demos," Alan Kay paid tribute to not only Engelbart but also English. According to Kay, English turned Engelbart's ideas from "something that was merely an opinion…into something that was much more understandable." This couldn't have been accomplished without "Bill English and his team of doers." English died of respiratory failure in San Rafael, California on July 26, 2020, at the age of ninety-one.

GEORGE WHITESIDES

1939–PRESENT

Field | Chemistry
Major Contribution | Has made discoveries in organometallic chemistry, soft lithography, microfluidics and nanotechnology.
Kentucky Connection | Born and raised in Louisville

> *I, personally, take it as a matter of faith that curiosity is essential to science, for its ability to provide fresh ideas, for its requirement to think outside the limits of a particular profession, for its ability to hone the skill of observation, for its ability to provide a common way for people (including scientists) to wonder about the world they inhabit (and the worlds their grandchildren may later inhabit).*
>
> *—Whitesides in a 2018 essay titled "Curiosity and Science"*

GEORGE McCLELLAND WHITESIDES was born on August 3, 1939, in Louisville. His father was a chemical engineer who encouraged his son's scientific curiosity. As an example of the tolerance his parents had for childhood experimentation, Whitesides said that around the fourth grade, he heard somewhere that rubber melts when heated. He put this claim to the test by pouring some gasoline out of a lawnmower and into an old tire that was lying in the garage. He struck a match, and the tire caught on fire. So did the garage. The fire department came and put out the fire. When the smoke cleared, Whitesides wasn't punished; his parents never even mentioned it. And besides, Whitesides learned something from the incident: rubber tires burn but do not melt.

As a teenager, Whitesides's first job was as a lab assistant at his father's company. One of his favorite tasks was cleaning glassware, work that he found strangely "soothing." The experience drew him toward a career in chemistry. When asked about his enjoyment of such a mundane task, Whitesides explained: "Any profession consists of a lot of routine stuff and occasionally really interesting things. If you like the routine stuff, the whole thing is okay."

One of Whitesides's teachers recognized his ability and recommended to his parents that he attend the Phillips Academy, a private boarding school in Andover, Massachusetts, about twenty-fives miles north of Boston. Established in 1778, the Phillips Academy is one of the most elite schools in the country. Among its alumni are two U.S. presidents, several foreign heads of state, many members of Congress and five Nobel laureates. Although Whitesides had never heard of the school and didn't even know where New England was, he agreed to go.

After graduating in 1957, he stayed in Massachusetts to attend Harvard University. As a freshman, Whitesides was trying to decide on a major and narrowed the choice down to chemistry or mathematics. Although Whitesides claims he was a "perfectly adequate" mathematician, that apparently wasn't good enough for Harvard's math department, and his professors encouraged him to pursue other interests. So he turned to chemistry. But there was a problem: he was failing his analytical chemistry course. He asked what he could do. The professor replied: "Well, I guess you'll have to learn the material." And so he did. In a few weeks' time, Whitesides mastered the material, aced the final exam and earned an A for the course. It was just the beginning of a brilliant career.

Before graduating from Harvard in 1960, Whitesides won a National Science Foundation fellowship for graduate study at any university. He applied to the University of California at Berkeley, but for some reason, the school never responded to his application or follow-up inquiries. It turned out to be a fortuitous turn of events, because Whitesides ended up at the California Institute of Technology in Pasadena, where he worked under the imminent chemist John D. Roberts.

Roberts was a pioneer in using nuclear magnetic resonance (NMR) spectroscopy, a technique used to identify molecules and analyze their structure. Roberts trained Whitesides on how to use the NMR spectrometer. But time on the machine during daylight hours was scarce, so Whitesides spent many late nights on the apparatus listening to folk music on the radio. He later recalled the entire process as being "just great fun."

What was Whitesides doing? He was using the results from NMR spectroscopy to do density matrix calculations. Density matrices are mathematical constructs that can describe the quantum state of a system. Whitesides was applying the matrix technique to study Grignard reagents, chemical compounds constructed from three components: the metal magnesium, a chemical from the periodic table's halogen group and an organic molecule. Looking back, Whitesides recalled: "I did density matrix calculations in a period when organic chemists not only did not do density matrix calculations but had never heard of a density matrix." Indeed, even Roberts learned about density matrices from Whitesides.

Whitesides wrote up his research and turned in his dissertation. In the acknowledgements, he thanked Roberts for his allowing him to pursue his own interests. Whitesides explained: "There was an enormous amount of autonomy in the group. People could basically do what they wanted to do." He later used the same approach with his own research group, claiming that things do not run well if the director is the only source for ideas. "Had I been raised in a different research group in which the expectation was that all ideas come from the research director, I would have started from a different point. Where I would have ended up, I don't know."

After earning his doctorate in chemistry from Caltech, Whitesides skipped the usual step of seeking a postdoctoral position and immediately became an assistant professor at the Massachusetts Institute of Technology. He began the new job in September 1963, although his doctorate wasn't officially conferred until 1964 because Caltech awarded degrees once a year. During his early years at MIT, Whitesides shared lab space with students; an actual office would have to wait four to five years.

From the very beginning of his teaching career, Whitesides promoted a collegial atmosphere within his research group. "Nobody ever said that you worked 'for' George Whitesides; you worked 'with' him," said chemist Charles P. Casey, Whitesides' first graduate student and now emeritus professor at the University of Wisconsin. "He was always trying to get people to take ownership of their problems, to come up with their own ideas of what to do next, and to encourage that kind of independence." Milan Mrksich, a former postdoctoral student who is now a professor of chemistry at the University of Chicago, said of Whitesides: "He does a great job of bringing out the best in each of his coworkers. He's clearly the smartest person in the group and the person with the best intuition and the broadest knowledge of many areas of science and engineering."

Shortly after joining the faculty at MIT, Whitesides was invited to join a biotechnology project in the chemical engineering department. It turned out that the project organizers couldn't convince any of MIT's biochemists to take part. Young, curious and eager, Whitesides accepted the invitation. The project gave him a chance to work with biologists and learn the field. The experience would lay the foundation for Whitesides's later interdisciplinary research on using enzymes for organic synthesis, the development of biocompatible surfaces and the creation of microfluidic devices for cell biology. (Microfluidics is the study of fluid behavior at scales less than a millimeter. At this scale, factors such as surface tension, energy dissipation and fluid resistance become dominant.)

Whitesides's primary research interest at MIT was in surface chemistry. His group began by looking at polyethylene surfaces. That work eventually led to research on soft lithography, a technique that can create microscopic patterns or formations on surfaces. This, in turn, led to micro-contact printing, in which soft lithography is used to create stamps that can transfer patterns to a surface in much the same way that stamps can transfer ink onto paper. Over time, soft lithography and micro-contact printing have become standard techniques in engineering and materials science. He is also credited with helping develop an organic chemical reaction that bears his name: the Corey-House-Posner-Whitesides reaction.

During his years at MIT, Whitesides met his future wife, Barbara, who was working as an editor at the university. She had graduated from Harvard and earned a doctorate in English literature from Rutgers University. The couple would eventually have two sons, George Thomas and Ben. George Thomas chose a career in space exploration. He was the longtime CEO of Virgin Galactic, a company that designs and builds spacecraft, and was chief of staff at NASA. Ben is a songwriter and lead singer for the Joggers, an indie rock band based in Portland, Oregon. Their father enjoys classical music and plays the classical guitar, a hobby that may have played a role, albeit unintentionally, in Ben's career choice. A proponent of freedom and autonomy in leading a research group, Whitesides had a similar approach to raising his sons. According George Thomas, "My father's fundamental philosophy toward child rearing was that kids need to figure it out for themselves."

In 1982, after nineteen years at MIT, Whitesides moved down the street to Harvard University, his alma mater. What prompted the move? With a focus on solving practical problems, Whiteside's research style fit in perfectly at MIT. Whitesides said that he needed a "change in scenery." Eventually, Whitesides was awarded one of only twenty-five University Professorships. The title of University Professor is an honor bestowed on faculty whose scholarship and professional achievements have attained the highest order. The honor was created in 1935 for those "working on the frontiers of knowledge, and in such a way as to cross the conventional boundaries of the specialties."

Whitesides is the director of the Whitesides Research Group at Harvard, a group of mostly postdoctoral scientists occupying a six-thousand-square-foot lab. The goal of the group is ambitious: "to fundamentally change the paradigms of science." The group uses chemistry as an entry point into other disciplines such as optics, electronics or biology. According to John Rogers, an engineering professor at the University of Illinois who worked in the research group, "Chemistry was the core expertise that provided the competitive advantage, but there was no sense of chemistry as a narrowly defined discipline. It was chemistry to solve problems, not necessarily to do chemistry." Whitesides chose research problems that are important and useful in the real world. "We don't make a clear distinction between science and technology," he said. "We try to make a distinction between good and bad or well done and poorly done."

Whitesides changed the focus of his research repeatedly throughout his career, averaging about ten years in a particular area. The scientific community did not always welcome these career shifts. "If you have spent the first twenty years of your career working on x and you try to move to y, the community will usually kill you," Whitesides claimed. Sometimes he's been asked by younger chemists if he's related to the George Whitesides who used to do organometallic chemistry. According to fellow Harvard chemist Jeremy Knowles, "He has the fundamental creative fearlessness of a real experimental scientist" and is "one of the most eclectic scientists I know." Mark Wrighton, who knew Whitesides at MIT, said: "George is willing to dive into areas where he doesn't know a lot and to invest the time needed to learn and understand the critical issues that need to be addressed." Whitesides knows it's time to change his research focus when the area becomes crowded with scientists. "Unless we're doing something that is different from what other people can do, I don't see any reason we should be doing it," Whitesides explained. In his later career, Whitesides's research interests turned toward big-picture problems such as the origin of life and complexity, which he defines as systems with interacting components.

Whitesides has been issued 162 patents and co-founded over a dozen companies worth over $20 billion. His interest in companies is a manifestation of his problem-solving approach to science. "I think universities have an obligation to try to make what they do real," he argued. According to Whitesides, universities and industries play complementary roles in improving society. "To say that there should be no contact between the two is crazy, and to say that the two should be fused is crazy," he said. "It should be a good marriage." Although an eager entrepreneur, Whitesides has this sober warning about the American free-market system:

"Capitalism is a wonderful economic engine, but it assigns little value to long-term projects or societal problems."

An example of one of the companies Whitesides has been involved with is the nonprofit Diagnostics for All. The company's mission is to create diagnostics for the developing world that are cheap, portable and easy to use. One diagnostic tool, made from patterned paper, is the size of a postage stamp. Microfluidic channels printed on the paper lead to tiny chemical reservoirs. When the paper is wetted with a bodily fluid such as blood or urine, the fluid makes its way through the channels, interacting with the chemicals in the reservoirs, and the paper turns different colors, revealing the diagnosis. The tests are inexpensive, portable and don't require electricity, clean water or a doctor. The tool can test for liver function, cholesterol level and diabetes.

Besides his scientific research, Whitesides has been very active in public service. He has served on advisory committees for NASA, the National Science Foundation and the Department of Defense. Since 1984, he has served on the National Research Council in a variety of capacities. In 2002, he served as chair of the panel that evaluated the state of chemical research in the United Kingdom. The findings were summarized in what became known as the Whitesides Report. In 2007, he served on the committee that wrote *Rising Above the Gathering Storm*, a report that examined U.S. competitiveness in science and technology.

Whitesides has also tried to communicate his science to the layperson. In 1997, Whitesides, in collaboration with photographer Felice Frankel, published a book titled *On the Surfaces of Things*. The book brings Whitesides's science to a general audience through the use of cutting-edge photographic technology.

Whitesides has a singularly impressive list of accomplishments. He is the author of over 1,300 scientific papers and articles. He ranked fifth on a list of the most cited chemists from 1981 to 1997 and thirty-eighth on the same list from 2000 through 2010. According to the Hirsch index, a ranking that combines the number of published papers with the number of citations of those papers by other scientists, Whitesides was the most influential living chemist in 2011. Whitesides's scientific accomplishments have been recognized by forty-nine awards and prizes. Today, Whitesides continues his research at Harvard.

ROBERT GRUBBS

1942–2021

Field | Chemistry
Major Accomplishment | Won the Nobel Prize for chemistry in 2005
for the development of the metathesis method in organic synthesis
Kentucky Connection | Born in Marshall County and raised in Paducah

> *One of my colleagues and I look at each other regularly and say, "We have the world's best job."*
>
> *—Grubbs in a YouTube video*

ROBERT GRUBBS was born in a place formerly known as Howard's Grove in Marshall County, Kentucky, on February 27, 1942. In a 2005 interview with the *Paducah Sun*, Grubbs claimed that the little community "lost its identity when the grade school fell down" so he now gives his birthplace as "near Possum Trot."

Grubbs was the middle child, sandwiched between two sisters. According to Grubbs's Nobel Prize autobiography, Grubbs's father, Howard, was a mechanic. As a child, Grubbs remembered helping him rebuild car engines, install plumbing and build houses. After Howard served two years in the army during World War II, he moved the family to Paducah, where he took night classes to become a diesel mechanic. Howard then got a job working for the Tennessee Valley Authority (TVA) operating and maintaining the heavy equipment used to build dams.

Grubbs's mother, Faye Atwood, the daughter of a strawberry farmer, was a teacher. As a child, Faye was sickly and couldn't help with the farm, so they sent her to college, where she received her teaching license after two years. She taught school for thirty-five years, starting with a little one-room schoolhouse teaching all the grades and ending at Farley Elementary School, where she taught first grade. Some of Grubbs's earliest memories are of tagging along with her to school when the babysitter couldn't make it and of attending evening and weekend classes with her while she worked toward her bachelor's degree. It took Faye twenty-eight years, but she finally earned her degree. "She taught us the importance of an education," Grubbs recalled. "The academic model of my mother and grandmother and the very practical, mechanical training from my father turned out to be perfect training for organic chemical research."

One of Grubbs' sisters, Bonnie Berry, still lives in Paducah and agreed that their mother was a positive influence on their intellectual lives. "She always encouraged us to read," Bonnie remembered. "We didn't have television back then, so it gave us something to do. Reading and learning was just part of our lives." But Bonnie never sensed there was anything special about her brother. "In fact," she joked, "I was afraid I was going to have to take care of him all of his life."

As a child, Grubbs enjoyed building things. "We got five cents a week allowance, and we'd pool our money and go buy nails," Bonnie recalled. "We'd get some old scraps of wood and just began nailing them together. We wanted to see what we could make." Afterward, they would dismantle their constructions, saving the nails for another day. According to Grubbs, "My mother always claimed that my spending my money on nails instead of on candy was why I was so skinny as a kid."

A childhood friend, Jerry McGregor, grew with Grubbs on Lieberman Street on the south side of Paducah. According to McGregor, Grubbs "was a normal kid who liked to have fun. We used to camp out in his yard, play basketball and stickball. We did all of the normal things that kids did back then."

Grubbs's interest in science was sparked in junior high school by his teachers, most notably his science teacher, Louise Barnreuther. (Author's note: I also had Mrs. Barnreuther for science, and I mowed her lawn.) "She was just a natural teacher who challenged us, who let us do creative things in class," Grubbs remembered. "She would say things that were wrong in class and see if we caught it and come back the next day to challenge her on it. She just pulled all of those kind of things, which were really, really important. I think that's where it [science] got my attention." At the time in the 1950s, Paducah was home to what was known as the "atomic plant," a giant uranium enrichment facility. Thus, there were many scientists who lived in the area and who no doubt insisted on quality schools. In fact, Mrs. Barnreuther had worked there. "I got a good education because I was encouraged to work hard and learn without getting burned out," Grubbs declares.

Grubbs attended Tilghman High School, where he graduated with honors in 1960. According to Bonnie, as a teenager, Grubbs was six foot six but weighed only 125 pounds. "We called him Goose," she said. He played basketball but was the team's lowest scorer, managing only three points for the entire season. He was better at track and field, where he competed as a high jumper. According to Bonnie, "He was good at the high jump because he was skin and bones and all legs." As a senior, he was the track team's third-highest scorer.

After high school, Grubbs attended the University of Florida, where he initially majored in agricultural chemistry, a field that combined his interest in science with his experience in farming. During the summer, he worked at an animal nutrition laboratory where he analyzed cattle feces. A friend was working in an organic chemistry laboratory at the university, and he invited Grubbs to come help in the evenings. There, he enjoyed making new molecules, which he found "even more fun than building houses," and the organic chemicals smelled better than cow poop. The laboratory was under the direction of a new faculty member named Merle Battiste, and Grubbs switched majors to organic chemistry and join Battiste's research group. Battiste trained Grubbs to be a productive organic chemistry researcher.

Grubbs remembered reading an influential textbook titled *Mechanisms and Structure in Organic Chemistry* by E.S. Gould from which he learned how organic chemical reactions take place. He was fascinated at the prospect of doing simple chemical transformations that revealed how reactions happened. According to Grubbs, "This direct coupling of simple observations with fundamental chemical reactions is the power of organic chemistry."

Grubbs earned his bachelor of science degree in 1963 and stayed on to earn a master's degree in 1965. At that point, Battiste suggested Grubbs switch to another university to work with a different research group and broaden his training. Grubbs agreed, but just before leaving, Grubbs heard a lecture by a young Australian chemist named Rolli Pettit, who talked about the use of transition metals in organic chemistry. Grubbs would pursue this area of research in the coming years.

Grubbs chose Columbia University, where he worked under Professor Ronald Breslow. This was no accident; Florida's Battiste had been Breslow's first doctoral student. According to Grubbs, "It was an exciting time in the Breslow group," which "provided an amazingly stimulating environment." Grubbs did his research on a chemical called cyclobutadiene and completed his doctorate in 1968.

During his second year at Columbia, Grubbs met his future wife, Helen O'Kane, a speech pathologist from Brooklyn. The couple would have three children: Barney (1972), Brendan (1974), and Kathleen (1977). Barney followed in his father's footsteps and became a professor of chemistry, Brendan pursued a career in medicine and Kathleen earned her doctorate in clinical psychology.

After Columbia, Grubbs spent a year as a postdoctoral fellow working with James Collman at Stanford University. There, Grubbs turned his attention toward organometallic chemistry, a field that was in its infancy and thus provided a rich variety of research opportunities. According to Grubbs, "There appeared to be an incredible array of important catalytic processes emerging in the field while little was known about the fundamental transformation involved." Collman developed a way of looking at the different reactions that served as a basis for understanding the steps in the catalytic processes. One of the most interesting of these was olefin metathesis, a process that required completely new steps to understand.

In 1969, Grubbs joined the faculty at Michigan State University (MSU), the only school that offered him a position. There, he began his independent research on olefin metathesis and other areas of catalysis. Grubbs was welcomed into a supportive environment at MSU and called his time there "very productive." Among his many excellent students was Akira Miyashita, a postdoctoral fellow who introduced new techniques to the research group and modeled an outstanding work ethic. After nine years at MSU, Grubbs accepted a position at the prestigious California Institute of Technology. Miyashita moved to Pasadena with Grubbs and helped him reestablish his research group.

In October 2005, Grubbs got the call informing him that he and two other chemists had been awarded the Nobel Prize. "Sure I was surprised," Grubbs admitted in an interview with the *Paducah Sun*. "You hear rumors, but never know that you're even being considered for a Nobel Prize. It is exciting, because you don't expect things like this to happen." As a kid growing up in Paducah, Grubbs admitted that "back then I wasn't even sure what the Nobel Prize was."

Grubbs won the Nobel Prize "for the development of the metathesis method in organic synthesis." OK, so what does that mean? First, organic substances are chemicals that contain the element carbon—the basis of all life on Earth. Synthesis is the construction of complex chemicals from simpler ones. So "organic synthesis" involves the intentional construction in the laboratory of organic chemicals. Metathesis, which means "changing places," is an important type of chemical reaction in the process of organic synthesis. In metathesis, double bonds between carbon atoms are broken and reorganized, allowing groups of atoms to move around and change place. This chemical juggling results in new molecules with new properties.

Around 1992, Grubbs discovered a metallic compound based on the element ruthenium, a rare transition metal. The compound helps the metathesis reaction go faster; in chemical jargon, it acts as a catalyst. The new "Grubbs catalyst" had several advantages over previous catalysts. First, Grubbs's ruthenium-based catalyst is stable in air. Also, the Grubbs catalyst had the advantage of working selectively on a molecule's double carbon bonds without disturbing the bonds between other atoms in the molecule. Finally, the new catalyst worked in the presence of water, alcohol, and carboxyl acids. Grubbs's discovery paved the way for practical applications in the areas of plastics and pharmaceuticals. It also contributed to the rise of "green chemistry" that reduces the volume of hazardous waste in chemical manufacturing.

Left: A Ruthenium crystal. Grubbs discovered a chemical catalyst based on this element. *Shutterstock*.

Right: Ruthenium is a chemical element with the symbol Ru and atomic number 44. It is a rare transition metal belonging to the platinum group. *Shutterstock*.

A tree-lined walk on the campus of the California Institute of Technology (Caltech). *Shutterstock.*

During his career, Grubbs served as a scientific mentor to several hundred graduate students and postdoctoral fellows in his research group. In his Nobel Prize autobiography, Grubbs said: "They have all left their mark. I thank them all for their hard work, for their creative contributions and for making chemistry fun."

Robert Grubbs died on December 19, 2021, at age seventy-nine. The cause of death was a heart attack suffered while he was being treated for lymphoma.

PHILLIP SHARP

1944-PRESENT

Field | Biology
Major Contribution | Won the 1993 Nobel Prize for Physiology or
  Medicine for his discovery of split genes
Kentucky Connection | Born and raised in Falmouth, graduated from
  Union College in Barbourville

> *Kentucky taught me how to work. There's nothing that
> focuses your mind like a day in the hot sun working in
> a field. You know to put your head down, keep moving
> forward, and don't complain. That lesson has been useful.*
>
> *—Sharp in a 2018 YouTube video*

PHILLIP ALLEN SHARP was born in the northern Kentucky town of
Falmouth on June 6, 1944, the same day that Allied forces landed on the
beaches of Normandy. His ancestors had lived in the area for over one
hundred years. His father, Joseph Walter Sharp, was a tenant farmer, and
his mother was Kathrin Colvin Sharp. Both parents came from big families,
so Sharp grew up in the company of many relatives. When Sharp was seven
years old, the family bought a small farm on a bend in the Licking River
near McKinneysburg.

About farm life, Sharp said, "I enormously enjoyed the feeling of being
outside, of being among that noise and diversity....It's overwhelmingly

beautiful to me." But there was plenty of work to be done on a farm. Sharp helped milk the cows and feed the pigs. For a few years, the farm had horses, and Sharp had the experience of plowing a field behind a team of horses. Sharp learned a lot from observing the farm animals. In an interview on a YouTube video, Sharp claims that he "could recognize so many human traits in animal behavior and their emotional state that it became very clear that there was a continuum in the way the brain works between animals and humans and you could see behaviors that were quite similar." These casual observations raised questions in his mind about biology and evolution.

Phillip Sharp wearing a medal symbolizing one of the many scientific prizes he has won. *Conrad Erb/Science History Institute/Wikimedia Commons.*

Sharp also learned from the plant life in and around the farm. He observed the enormous variety of plants encompassing everything from weeds to crops to trees and everything in between. Sharp recalled that introducing hybrid crops resulted in increased yields and remembered talking to his father about what exactly a hybrid was. They understood the seeds couldn't be planted again because they wouldn't germinate, but neither he nor his father could explain this behavior. Nevertheless, it illustrated how plants could be shaped by human selection and breeding. This helped Sharp become comfortable with the idea that biotechnology could create new products.

Sharp was educated in the public schools of Pendleton County, attending Butler Grade School and Pendleton County High School. In his Nobel Prize autobiography, Sharp claimed: "Even though my studies never interfered with sports or fun, I managed to gain an appreciation of math and science." He was strong in math but poor in English. And "conduct was never my high point." When he entered the sixth grade, Sharp became interested in science. "Anything about science fascinated me," he recalled. He talked to friends about science and read popular science books. His teachers took note and directed him into accelerated classes.

In high school, a math teacher and a chemistry/physics teacher took an interest in Sharp and encouraged his interest in science. Sharp's intellectual curiosity turned away from the biology he had observed on the farm and toward mathematics, chemistry and physics. Why? Because, as Sharp explained in an interview, high school biology was taught by rote memory and was "terribly uninteresting." The problem was there were no general principles that seemed to apply to what he was learning. In contrast, in chemistry, he could learn a few rules and equations and use them to understand an enormous amount of science. What would eventually lead him back into biology were broad and powerful principles in molecular and cell biology that enabled him to understand a whole range of phenomena, including human beings. It wouldn't be until after he earned his doctorate that he would turn once again toward biology.

Sharp graduated from high school at the top of his class. When Sharp was only six years old, his parents had discussed college with him. They encouraged him to save up his money so that he could attend. So Sharp raised cattle and grew tobacco and put the proceeds from his sales in the bank. The money eventually paid for about a year and a half of college. Because of his upbringing, Sharp was more comfortable at a small college in a rural setting, so he attended Union College, a small eight-hundred-student private institution in Barbourville, a town in southeastern Kentucky in the heart of Appalachia. The area was poverty-stricken, and many of the children were malnourished. Sharp claimed that half of the young men from the area drafted to fight in the Vietnam War failed their physical. Sharp said that Union College "was one of the gateways for the youth from the mountains in the eastern part of the state to emerge into a larger world." At Union, he majored in chemistry and mathematics and met his future wife, Ann Holcomb, a coed from New Jersey who was studying to become an elementary teacher. The couple got married in 1964.

In his junior year at Union College, Sharp befriended a new chemistry professor named Dan Foote, who had earned his doctorate from the University of Illinois. Sharp spent most of his junior and senior years in Foote's classes, learning both organic and inorganic chemistry. Foote encouraged him to apply for graduate study in chemistry at Illinois. Sharp thought the idea of getting paid to study chemistry was "fabulous." This was during the post-Sputnik era, which meant plenty of federal money was available to support graduate students in the sciences. Sharp was offered a fellowship; he accepted and was soon a student at one of the top chemistry departments in the country. He flunked most of the entrance exams because he hadn't had the material, so he spent his first semester taking the senior-level classes to get caught up.

Soon, he was working alongside his doctoral advisor, Victor Bloomfield, in physical chemistry. According to Sharp, Bloomfield, a newly arrived professor from the West Coast, was an excellent mentor who "broadened my perspective on society and culture by being a long-haired liberal, well-read and artistic friend." Bloomfield also made sure Sharp attended national scientific meetings, got exposure and made connections. Over three years, they published several scientific papers together. Sharp finished work on his doctorate in 1969. His thesis dealt with the description of DNA as a polymer using statistical and physical theories. Sharp admitted that his "attempts at experimental science at this stage were juvenile." He added that although he was raised on a farm, "I was never very skilled in manual tasks; in fact, I soon lost interest in any complex 'hands-on' manipulation."

As he contemplated his scientific future, Sharp didn't think the problems that chemistry presented to him were interesting, so he turned his attention toward biology. In 1968, he read a volume titled *The Genetic Code*, which gave the results of a symposium held in 1966 at Cold Spring Harbor, a laboratory on Long Island. The book focused on the structure of DNA, how long the molecule was and how much genetic material it held. As he read and studied more about DNA and genetics, he decided to make the transition from chemistry into what is now known as molecular biology. Sharp thought he could use molecular biology and DNA as a way of understanding more about the thought processes and health of human beings. The field offered new territory for scientific exploration and discovery. Sharp would have to learn some biology and biochemistry, but his solid background in chemistry gave him the tools he would need to do that. In fact, Sharp had only one formal college-level biology class in his life, and that was general biology back at Union College.

His next step was to find a postdoctoral position that would match his new interests. Sharp wrote a letter of inquiry to Norman Davidson, a professor at Caltech who was a physical chemist transitioning to biology, similar to the change Sharp wanted to make. Sharp had read his scientific papers and found them fascinating. Luckily, Davidson said yes, and Sharp moved his family to Pasadena. He knew that at Caltech, he would be among the best scientists in the world. If he could hold his own and make contributions at Caltech, he could make contributions anywhere.

At Caltech, Sharp was interested in learning more about the chemistry of DNA and how to use DNA to look at a gene. He started using an electron microscope to look at the mapping of genes on chromosomes, a technique that was totally new. The idea was, if you can see it, you can understand it. And then you can manipulate it. Specifically, Sharp studied plasmids, a genetic structure in cells that can replicate independently of the chromosomes.

When his postdoc period was over at Caltech, Sharp looked for a job but couldn't find one. The year was 1971: the economy was poor, and few academic positions were available. He had several interviews but no offers. In hindsight, the lack of an offer opened up a new opportunity. Sharp decided to look for a second postdoctoral position and wrote to Nobel laureate James Watson, the director of Cold Spring Harbor Laboratory (CSHL). Watson had discovered, with Francis Crick, the double-helical structure of DNA. Watson offered Sharp a position, and he accepted. Sharp wanted to work with viruses, and CSHL gave him an opportunity to do that.

By 1974, Sharp was getting job offers from institutions around the country, but he was waiting for a call from MIT, mainly because he wanted to work with David Baltimore, who would win the Nobel Prize in 1975 and was working in virology. Sharp had learned about Baltimore while at Caltech and knew him to be a dynamic and charismatic scientist who had good people working around him. After waiting six months, Sharp got a call from another Nobel laureate, Salvador Luria, inviting him to come work at the recently established Center for Cancer Research (now the Koch Institute for Integrative Cancer Research) at MIT. Luria was the director of the center and, according to Sharp, "was a visionary who protected his young faculty from unnecessary interruptions, thus allowing their research programs to flourish in an ideal scientific environment." Sharp accepted the offer and moved into an office on the fifth floor that he shared with Baltimore and other top-notch scientists. The scientists would have a "floor meeting" every week to discuss their work.

Sharp moved his family to Newton, Massachusetts, a suburb of Boston about seven miles west of downtown. The family was growing. The couple's first child, a daughter named Christine, had been born in 1968 while Sharp was still in graduate school. A second daughter, Sarah, followed in 1974 just before the move to MIT and a third daughter, Helena, would follow in 1981. Sharp's wife, Ann, taught preschool.

The ultimate goal at MIT was to attack the problem of diseases like cancer. But this required understanding the fundamental processes at work in cells, genes and DNA. Sharp's focus was on these basic processes, and MIT had the resources and the critical mass of scientists needed to tackle big, complex problems. Biologists understood that there was a process by which genetic material is transferred from the cell nucleus to the rest of the cell. Sharp wanted to understand that process and suspected it was different for multicellular organisms than for single-celled creatures. By comparing this transfer of information to the structure of the gene, Sharp discovered our genes were split, meaning that the information transferred in our genes is broken up into little pieces and then reassembled in the larger cell as it is being transferred from the nucleus. He called this process RNA splicing and literally saw it happen using an electron microscope. Sharp made the discovery in 1977 over a six-month period.

The implications of Sharp's discovery were almost immediate. It was now clear that genetic mutations, the cause of many diseases, interfered with the process of RNA splicing. This explained why many human disease genes were defective. Soon, Sharp's colleague Robert Weinberg isolated the first human oncogene, a gene that causes cancer, and discovered that it came in pieces as predicted. Then scientists discovered viruses were hijacking the RNA splicing process and making tumor cells.

The next steps in Sharp's research were twofold. First, he wanted to understand the chemistry of RNA splicing. Second, he wanted to figure out the chemistry behind how genes were turned on and off, a process known as gene expression. For example, the difference between a skin cell and a blood cell is which genes are turned on and off. Similarly, the difference between a tumor cell and a healthy cell is which genes are turned on and off. These topics occupied Sharp for the next twenty years.

Sharp's scientific life almost took an unexpected detour in 1990. MIT was looking for a new president, and Sharp was asked to co-chair a faculty committee to assist in the search for a successor. As the process unfolded, it became clear that Sharp himself would make an excellent candidate. Sharp was offered the job, felt obligated to take it and initially said yes. But he began to have doubts about his decision. In an interview, Sharp admitted that he "hadn't thought through what my emotional state would be if I had to give up science." And that was the choice. He couldn't be the president of MIT and continue with his scientific career; it was one or the other. Sharp ultimately decided that he wouldn't be happy and fully committed to the job, so he changed his mind. Sharp later called it the biggest mistake of his life and regrets that his decision "cast a negative shadow on MIT for a while."

By the early 1990s, Sharp had received many prizes in recognition of his discoveries and knew he was being considered for the Nobel Prize. One October morning in 1993, he got the call from Sweden that all scientists hope to get. He had won the Nobel Prize in Physiology or Medicine for his discovery of split genes. He shared the prize with Richard Roberts, a British

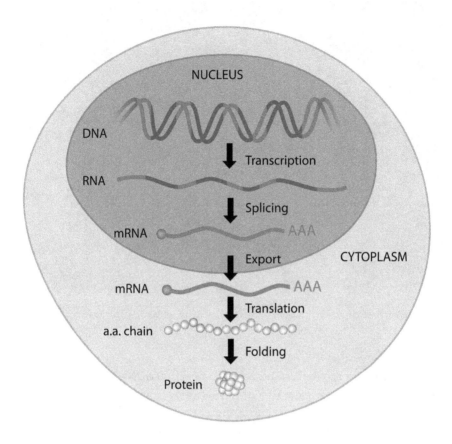

One of Sharp's research areas was gene expression, outlined in the diagram. *Shutterstock.*

biochemist. When the prize was announced, Sharp reacted by saying it "was pretty good for a Kentucky boy." In December, Sharp journeyed to Sweden, accompanied by his proud parents, to accept the award.

The reaction from Kentucky was swift. Back in his hometown, the middle school was renamed Phillip Sharp Middle School. The school is located at 35 Wright Road in Butler, Kentucky, and sits at the end of the road that Sharp lived on as a boy. When the renaming was announced, one of Sharp's colleagues told him, "Phillip, you can't mess up because you're gonna let down all those kids if you do."

Sharp claims he has always had a practical side, so it shouldn't be surprising that, besides his scientific work, he has been active in the entrepreneurial world. In 1978, he co-founded Biogen (now Biogen Idec), the third

An aerial view of the MIT campus on the Charles River in Cambridge, Massachusetts. Sharp was offered the presidency of MIT but decided against it. *Shutterstock.*

biotechnology company established in the United States. The company, headquartered on the edge of the MIT campus, has produced a plethora of therapeutics, including isolating the genes for the Hepatitis B vaccine, Alpha interferon used to treat cancer and Avonex and Tysabri, treatments for multiple sclerosis. In 2002, he helped found Alnylam Pharmaceuticals, another biotech company that focused on developing RNA Interference (RNAi), a new type of therapeutic agent. Sharp also co-founded Magen Biosciences in 2009, a company specializing in products for the skin, although his involvement was minimal.

In 2000, Sharp was made the founding director of MIT's McGovern Institute, a position that he held until 2004. A research institute focused on neuroscience, the McGovern Institute's mission is to understand the brain and apply that knowledge to the treatment of brain disorders. Sharp's primary jobs were organizing the institute, constructing the building, and recruiting faculty.

One of Sharp's doctoral students, Andrew Fire, won the 2006 Nobel Prize for Physiology or Medicine for his discovery of RNA Interference. Dozens of Sharp's former students run labs, direct companies or hold prestigious positions in universities and hospitals around the world.

Sharp used his Nobel Prize money to buy an old Federal-style house. He said that he and his family love New England and "enjoy its rural towns, coastal beauty, and the changes of seasons." He is currently an Institute Professor at MIT, the highest academic title awarded to faculty. Usually, only twelve MIT professors can hold this title at any time. Institute professors have complete freedom in their research and are free from teaching and other normal responsibilities. As of this writing, Sharp has published over four hundred scientific papers.

EUGENIA WANG

1945–PRESENT

Field | Genetics

Major Contribution | Has made important discoveries about how genetics effects aging

Kentucky Connection | Professor at the University of Louisville from 2000 until the present

> *I was fortunate to have my parents who, even in a very tight and stressed state when we first moved from mainland China to Taiwan after the World War II, allowed me to ask crazy questions and did not stifle me and say "Do not ask the question."*
>
> —*Wang, in an interview on Kentucky Educational Television's* One to One *program*

EUGENIA WANG was born in Nanking, China, on February 26, 1945, during the Chinese Civil War. When she was three, fighting between the Communists and Nationalists broke out in Nanking. Wang, her mother and three siblings escaped on a train, leaving her father, a newspaper copy editor, behind. They lived as refugees, first in Hanyang and then Guangzhou, for nearly a year. Her father eventually reunited with the family, and they moved to Taipei, Taiwan. "When we arrived, we were poor. But then, everybody was poor, so it was OK," Wang recalled.

Wang spent her formative years in Taipei, growing up as a bit of a tomboy with dirty knees and grimy socks from playing in the streets. She recalls an incident, at about age twelve, that forecast her future. She had noticed how hard her mother worked to prepare three family meals every day. And she had heard of a new powdered drink mix called Tang that NASA was planning for use by astronauts. Suddenly, she got an epiphany. "When I grow up, I'll be a scientist," she announced. "I will create three pills: a breakfast pill, a lunch pill, and a supper pill. And then you don't have to do any cooking, you don't have to do any grocery shopping." Wang's older sister had been listening and protested to her mother, "What kind of girl are you raising? I guarantee she will never find a husband. Who is the man who would want to marry her if she won't cook, she won't sew?" Wang responded with a rapid career switch: "Look, I'm going to be president; somebody else will do the sewing."

True to her adolescent declaration, when the time came to pick a career path, Wang chose science. In the post-Sputnik era, the sciences were a ticket to job security and upward mobility. So Wang took the intense two-day competitive national entrance exam to try to earn a spot at Taiwan National University. Only about one thousand of the top scoring students from tens of thousands of test-takers made the cut. Successful applicants would be assigned to an academic field based not on their interests but solely on their test scores. Wang didn't make the cut for her first choice, physics. But she earned a spot at the school and was placed into zoology, specifically, the field of entomology. Although it was not her preferred field, Wang felt lucky just to get into college. "It was everybody's dream at the time." She was awarded a scholarship but worked as a math tutor to help support the family. And so it was that Wang commenced her study of insects.

During her college years, Wang set into motion a plan to immigrate to America. "It was generally accepted that the U.S. had streets paved with gold," she recalled. On her own, she began learning English. She listened to the *Voice of America* on the radio, memorized the words in a Chinese-English dictionary and read English encyclopedias in the library.

When Wang graduated in 1966, she wanted to pursue graduate studies, but there were almost no graduate programs in Taiwan. Also, there were few opportunities for women to pursue their professions. So she put her immigration plan into action. She applied to graduate school in entomology at Northern Michigan University and was accepted. Then she borrowed $800 from one of her high school teachers and four of her father's friends, bought a ticket and made the move. After arriving in 1967, she continued to work on her English by watching the news and *The Johnny Carson Show* on television.

Wang earned her master's degree in 1969 and continued working toward a doctorate in entomology at Case Western Reserve University in Cleveland. And then a twist of fate occurred: her entomology adviser moved to Canada, and she had to switch into the lab of Bob Goldman, a cell biologist. It was fortuitous, because entomology, although a fascinating field, was not on the frontier of science. But the field of cell biology could lead into lots of different areas, including genetics. Goldman was studying the role of the cytoskeleton—an array of filaments made of protein that give the cell its shape—in cell movement and specialization. He suggested Wang investigate how the structures within a cell (called organelles) actually move. Wang's research found that the organelles can glide between the cell nucleus and the membrane along the protein filaments that form the cytoskeleton. She also discovered that a chemical called colchicine can cause the nucleus to move. At the time, the scientific consensus held that the cell nucleus was fixed in position—it did not move around within the cell. Such an important discovery prompted Goldman to convince Wang to present her findings at a meeting of the American Society for Cell Biology. Wang was understandably nervous about presenting; she was only a second-year graduate student, and English was her second language. "I think Bob Goldman made me rehearse every day for a month," she remembered. The talk went smoothly, but Wang said, "That really stirred up a storm in the lab."

Wang finished her doctorate in 1974 and won a fellowship from the National Institutes of Health that provided funding for her postdoctoral work. She ended up at Rockefeller University in New York City working with virologist Allan Goldberg. Unlike most universities, Rockefeller University is a small, private, research-focused graduate institution; there are no undergraduates. It is also an elite institution; some of the world's top scientists in biomedical research, including several Nobel laureates, work at Rockefeller. Wang knew nothing about viruses but was eager to learn. Her life, like most lives, was largely shaped by a series of accidents. "I got into entomology because of the circumstances of the exam. I came to the United States because of necessity, and I got into virology by accident, too," she observed.

Wang remained at Rockefeller for twelve years, and her research led her into the area for which she would earn an international reputation: aging. She began by resuming her study of cytoskeletal proteins but now looked at their behavior in cells that were infected by a virus. It was known that viral infection of a cell usually triggered the production of interferon, a protein involved in immune defense. Working with pioneering virologist Igor Tamm, Wang began investigating the effect of interferon on cell behavior. They got a surprising result. "We treated the cell with interferon, and all of a sudden [it] looked exactly flat down like a pancake," she remembered. Wang learned that the treated cells were behaving like they were in a state of senescence—cellular division had been halted. "That's how I got into aging," Wang explained.

Of course, being a woman in science had its own challenges. Wang recalled that every day at noon, all the male faculty and postdocs would adjourn to the university dining room for lunch, leaving the five female postdocs behind to eat by themselves. "It never occurred to them to invite us," she recalled. Then one day, a visiting female scientist noticed the lunchtime gender segregation and suggested that the women invite themselves to lunch. Wang gave it a try. She asked the professor in the neighboring lab, one of the friendlier faculty members, if he would mind if she and the other women joined him for lunch. "He said, 'Oh yeah, Eugenia, why not?'" And for the next eighteen months, Wang sat awkwardly through lunch without uttering a word. The problem was that although she had studied English, she wasn't confident in her ability to make small talk. When she finally worked up enough courage, she chatted easily about science, the weather and the news. Eventually, the men sought her out as a dining companion.

There were other small slights regarding Wang's gender. Once, a technician came to her lab to fix her electron microscope. Upon finishing, he asked if he could talk to Dr. Wang. "You have been talking to Dr. Wang for the last thirty minutes," she informed him. In another incident, she was visiting the University of Toronto to give a seminar. When she presented herself at the receptionist's desk at the university's guest housing in what turned out to be a men's dormitory, she was greeted with surprise. "You're Dr. Wang?" said the attendant. "Oh, no! We were expecting a man."

It was during her time at Rockefeller that Wang met and married computer scientist Alan Bloch, a native Kentuckian, thus laying to rest her older sister's long-ago concern about finding a husband. Soon, the couple had a son named Joseph. Now Wang faced the familiar female challenge of having to juggle a career with family responsibilities. She had one crucial advantage: her enlightened husband helped with the chores. During the week, they employed a babysitter to watch Joseph. On Saturdays, she took him to her lab, where he sat in his playpen while she did her experiments. When she went to a conference, she took Joseph along.

When Joseph was in first grade, his teacher asked him where lettuce came from. He confidently replied, "D'Agostino," the name of the gourmet grocery store the family frequented. Wang was embarrassed. "When my son couldn't recognize lettuce as a farm product, we realized we'd better get out of Manhattan," she joked. In 1987, Wang and her family left New York City, but not because Joseph was confused about the origins of lettuce. Wang was presented with an opportunity she couldn't refuse. McGill University in Montreal was establishing the new Bloomfield Centre for Research in Aging at the university's Lady Davis Institute for Medical Research and wanted Wang to be in charge of everything: fundraising, design of the facility and recruitment of faculty.

She accepted the job, and the family moved to Montreal. Besides running a lab, she had administrative responsibilities. Bloch took a part-time job as a computer engineer, which allowed him to spend more time at home with Joseph. And Bloch helped Wang with her scientific work by doing the statistical analysis of her data by computer. "He helps me formulate a lot of my thoughts, and he proofreads everything I write," she said. The marriage was a true partnership.

Hyman Schipper, a colleague of Wang's at McGill, once asked how she learned her administrative skills. Her surprising answer was that she read military biographies. She is a big fan of General Omar Bradley, the World War II general who ran the Veterans Administration after the war, helping soldiers transition back to civilian life. Reading about Bradley taught her a lot about managing people. "Bradley was a soldier's general," Wang said. "He knew what the foot soldiers need. Once you know what the foot soldier needs, you will be successful."

Wang takes care of her "foot soldiers." Atanu Duttaroy, a former postdoctoral student who worked in Wang's Montreal lab, recalled the day he arrived in Montreal with a rental truck full of his belongings. Wang told him she would meet him at his apartment. Duttaroy wondered to himself about the timing of the meeting because he had to get the truck unloaded. Duttaroy explained that to his surprise, "She, her husband and her son showed up, and believe it or not, they moved the stuff into my apartment."

Along with everything else, Wang continued her scientific research. Her lab was one of the first to discover that although senescent cells may have serious abnormalities, they do not die. Instead, they resist the process known as apoptosis, the programmed death of a cell. This led Wang to suggest that senescent cells play an important role in the development of age-related diseases such as cancer.

In 2000, the Wang gang moved again, this time to Louisville, her husband's hometown. She accepted a position as a professor in the Department of Biochemistry and Molecular Biology at the University of Louisville. A few years later, Wang became director of the newly established Gheens Center on Aging, part of the School of Medicine with funding from the Gheens Foundation, a local charitable organization. The center focuses on genetics and the biology of aging. Wang's own research continues to focus on the genetic mechanisms that cause predisposition to infectious diseases.

Of her scientific skills, Russell Prough, a University of Louisville biochemist who has worked with Wang, said that she can "look at data and make out a story as quick as anybody I've ever met." He added, "Her intuitions are so good that while [her research ideas] may look like leaps of faith, they normally always have potential for bearing fruit." Schipper gave this assessment of Wang: she is "extraordinarily tough" but fair and lives by "a powerful work ethic that abhors shortcuts and flimsy groundwork, and she really doesn't have much patience for individuals who are not ready to give their best to whatever they do.…Eugenia can be a tiger in the laboratory, [but] she's actually a pussycat outside of the workplace. She's extremely warm and sensitive; she cares tremendously about how people in her lab do long after they've left."

In a 2013 interview that aired on Kentucky Educational Television, Wang said that she feels great to be in Kentucky and that the bluegrass always makes her cry. When the interviewer asked why, she replied, "Because it's home."

J. RICHARD GOTT

1947–PRESENT

Field | Astrophysics
Major Contribution | Expert in the subjects of general relativity and
time travel
Kentucky Connection | Born and raised in Louisville

*We are not very powerful, and we have not been around
for very long. But we are intelligent creatures and we have
learned a lot about the universe and the laws that govern
it—how long ago it started, how its galaxies and stars
and planets formed. It is a stunning accomplishment.*

—J. Richard Gott writing at the end of
Welcome to the Universe

JOHN RICHARD GOTT III was born in Louisville on February 8, 1947, the only child of Dr. J. Richard Gott Jr. and Marjorie (Crosby) Gott. His father was a physician at the Veterans Administration Hospital, eventually becoming the chief of medicine and, later, the chief of staff. His mother did volunteer work in conservation and beautification. She was a member of myriad clubs and served a term as president of the Garden Club of Kentucky. The Garden Club was a cosponsor of the Floral Clock adorning the capitol grounds in Frankfort. On May 4, 1961, Marjorie dedicated the clock to "all Kentuckians who take pride in the beauty of their state."

J. Richard Gott is a professor of astrophysical sciences at Princeton University. He is noted for his contributions to cosmology and general relativity. *A. T. Service/ Wikimedia Commons.*

One of Marjorie's clubs would have a lasting influence on her son. As a college student, Marjorie was one of the founding members of the Louisville Astronomical Society, one of the most active and sophisticated organizations of its kind. The society had the use of an observatory with a twenty-one-inch reflecting telescope, held over forty public programs annually and had a branch of the society specifically for youth. In his early teens, Gott joined the Louisville Junior Astronomical Society and eventually became the editor of the society's publications. He also served a term as vice-president and president. Gott's involvement in the astronomical society no doubt played a pivotal role in his choice of career.

Gott attended Waggener High School in Louisville. The early sixties was the post-Sputnik era, and there was, according to Gott, "great energy and great excitement" surrounding the study of science and math in the schools. His teachers encouraged Gott's interests and told him about the Westinghouse Science Talent Search (now the Regeneron Science Talent Search), a research-based scientific competition for high school seniors. The competition began in 1942 and is the country's oldest and most prestigious science competition; many finalists enjoy distinguished careers in science, and about a dozen have won Nobel Prizes. Gott jumped at the opportunity to take part in the competition. He enjoyed geometry and decided on a research project where he would figure out potential crystalline structures. Gott's project won him a spot as a finalist for the competition.

Later in his career, during much of the 1980s and 1990s, Gott became a judge for the competition, an experience that gave him a chance to think about science education in America. "People sometimes wonder whether the quality of the best science students is going up or down," Gott said. "The answer is that it's the same high level." Gott has observed how "clusters" of semifinalists and finalists will pop up in particular schools. First, a school that has never had a finalist or semifinalist will have one. Then the next year, there might be two or three from the school. Gott's guess is that a talented teacher is responsible for the sudden increase. This also shows that there is "quite a lot of undiscovered scientific talent" waiting for a chance to blossom.

Gott's finalist status in the talent search presumably helped him get into Harvard University, where he studied physics. He graduated in 1969 and spent the summer in Europe, where he visited the Berlin Wall dividing democratic West Berlin from communist East Berlin. The wall was the first object for which Gott calculated a "survival time." The survival time is a statistical calculation for the time until a particular event occurs, such as a death in biology or a failure in engineering. Gott later applied the same analysis to calculate the survival time of everything from governments to Broadway plays. He has calculated the survival time for humanity, with 95 percent confidence, to be at least 5,100 years, but less than 7.8 million years. Gott admitted that's a wide range, but added it's a significant one. "The fate of our own species is extremely important to us," Gott said. "Some people predict we'll die out in the next hundred years if we aren't careful; others think we'll just last indefinitely. Neither is likely. In any case, we'd better not be complacent. The Earth is littered with the bones of extinct species."

In the fall of 1969, Gott began work toward a doctorate in astrophysics at Princeton University. After graduating in 1973, he won a postdoctoral fellowship at the California Institute of Technology and then a visiting fellowship at the University of Cambridge before returning to Princeton to join the astrophysics department in 1976. At Princeton, he developed an astrophysics course for non-science majors and created one of the country's first undergraduate courses on general relativity. Gott earned a reputation for great teaching and in 1998, won the President's Award for excellence in teaching.

In 1978, Gott married Lucy Jennifer Pollard (now known as Lucy Pollard-Gott), who holds a doctorate in psychology from Princeton and specializes in the psychology of the arts. She has published research on the structure of fairy tales, attribution theory and the novel and the poetry of Wallace Stevens. She has also written a popular book titled *The Fictional 100: Ranking the Most Influential Characters in World Literature and Legend*. The couple have a daughter, Elizabeth Marjorie Pollard-Gott.

One of Gott's first major scientific achievements dealt with the large-scale structure of the universe. At the time, there was a controversy over the distribution of galactic clusters throughout space. Were small high-density regions surrounded by vast low-density areas (astronomers call these "voids")? Or were voids in the middle of denser regions that resembled the structure of swiss cheese? Gott decided neither model was correct and proposed that instead, the universe had a sponge-like structure. This

Einstein–Rosen bridge
(wormhole)

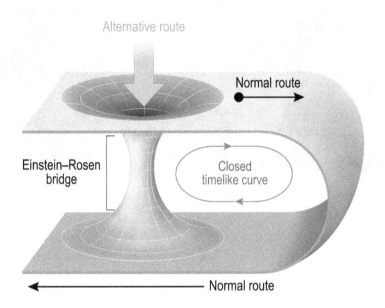

A wormhole (or Einstein-Rosen bridge) is a structure linking two points in spacetime. If they exist, wormholes could be a shortcut for space travelers. *Shutterstock.*

prediction has now been confirmed by telescopic observations. In 2016, Gott wrote a popular science book titled *The Cosmic Web: Mysterious Architecture of the Universe* that relates how he and other scientists figured out how the universe was arranged.

In 2005, Gott, along with his colleagues, used the Sloan Digital Sky Survey to create a "Map of the Universe," which was published in the *Astrophysical Journal* (vol. 624, no. 2 (May 2005): 463–84) and subsequently made its way into the popular press. The largest structure on the map, the "Sloan Great Wall of Galaxies," was, at the time, the largest structure ever found in the universe at 1.37 billion light years long. Gott got his name in the *Guinness Book of World Records* with that discovery.

A wormhole can be visualized as a tunnel through spacetime. *Shutterstock.*

Gott is a leading expert on the topic of Einstein's General Theory of Relativity. The General Theory is a new way to think about gravity. The theory says that gravity is caused by the bending or warping of spacetime around a massive object like the Sun. Because objects must travel through spacetime, if spacetime is curved, then the path an object takes through spacetime must also be curved. This new way of thinking opens up many possibilities, including the idea of a wormhole, a shortcut through spacetime.

Gott is most famous for his forays into one of the most fascinating topics in science: time travel. According to Einstein's Special Theory of Relativity, the faster you move through space, the slower you move through time. We know this effect as time dilation. It is not "just a theory"; it really happens. Subatomic particles called muons do in fact decay more slowly when they move at speeds approaching the speed of light. Time dilation also happens at low speeds, but the effect is much smaller. Cosmonaut Sergei Avdeyev, who orbited the Earth for 748 days during three space flights, is about one-fiftieth of a second younger than he would have been had he just stayed home. Thus, time travel into the future has already been accomplished, albeit to a tiny degree.

But can you travel backward in time? In 1985, Gott discovered a solution to Einstein's field equations for the gravitational field around one cosmic string. He followed that discovery up in 1991 with a solution for the gravitational field surrounding two moving cosmic strings. OK, but what's a cosmic string? According to the Big Bang theory, the universe began with an explosion of space that generated tremendous heat. If the conditions were just right, physicists think that strings of pure energy, millions of light years long and infinitesimally thin, may have survived in their origin state rather than cooling off with the rest of the universe. The strings would be unimaginably dense—a thousand trillion tons of mass for every inch of length. This gigantic mass would warp the surrounding space so that the space would act like a lens.

In an article in *Physical Review Letters*, Gott concluded that time travel might be achieved by bending such a cosmic string into a closed loop. In an article in *Time* magazine, he explained,

> *You could try to construct a cosmic-string time machine by finding a large loop of cosmic string and somehow manipulating it so it would contract rapidly under its own tension, like a rubber band. The extraordinary energy density of the string curves space-time sharply, and by flying a spaceship around the two sides of the loop as they pass each other at nearly the speed of light, you'd travel into the past.*

An aerial view of the campus of Princeton University at sunrise. *Shutterstock.*

In an equally intriguing possibility, Gott wrote in a scientific paper that if a time loop existed at the beginning of the universe, "It would be like having one branch of a tree circle around and grow up to be the trunk. In that way, the universe could be its own mother." So maybe the universe didn't come from nothing, maybe it came from something and that something was itself. While all this may sound like science fiction, according to popular science author John Gribbin, "Gott is a serious and respectable scientist whose work on time travel is absolutely mainstream and in line with the general theory of relativity." Gott wrote about these and other discoveries in his 2001 popular science book, *Time Travel in Einstein's Universe: The Physical Possibilities of Travel Through Time.*

In 2016, after forty years on the Princeton faculty, Gott retired and became an emeritus professor. Like everyone else, Gott has had to struggle with religious questions. "I'm a Presbyterian," Gott declared. "I believe in God; I always thought that was the humble position to take....I think if you want to know how the universe started, that's a legitimate question for physics. But if you want to know why it's here, then you may have to know—to borrow Stephen Hawking's phrase—the mind of God."

BIBLIOGRAPHY

Chapter 3: Ephraim McDowell

Gray, Laman, Sr., MD. *The Life and Times of Ephraim McDowell*. Danville, KY: Ephraim McDowell House, 1987.

Chapter 4: James Espy

Espy, James Pollard. *The Philosophy of Storms*. Boston: Little and Brown, 1841.
McDonald, J.E. "James Espy and the Beginnings of Cloud Thermodynamics." *Bulletin American Meteorological Society* 44, no. 10 (October 1963): 634–41. http://kirkmcd.princeton.edu/JEMcDonald/mcdonald_bams_44_634_63.pdf.
Morehead, L.M. *A Few Incidents in the Life of Professor James P. Espy*. Cincinnati, OH: Robert Clarke & Co., 1888.
"Sketch of James Pollard Espy." *Popular Science Monthly*, April 1889.

Chapter 5: Nathan Stubblefield

Lochte, Bob. *Kentucky Farmer Invents Wireless Telephone! But Was It Radio? Facts and Folklore About Nathan Stubblefield*. Murray, KY: All About Wireless, 2001.
———. "Lives of a Cell." Inc. Newsletter. https://www.inc.com/magazine/19961215/2030.html.

Chapter 6: John Thompson

Blumenthal, Karen. *Tommy: The Gun That Changed America*. New York: Roaring Brook Press, 2015.

Crawford-Lackey, Katie, and Christopher Beebout. "Tommygun Inventor." ExploreKYHistory, June 26, 2021. https://exploreekyhistory.ky.gov/items/show/540.

Koch, Jacob. "Our Rich History: John T. Thompson of Newport Was a Firearms Inventor of International Acclaim." *Northern Kentucky Tribune*, January 6, 2020. https://www.nkytribune.com/2020/01/our-rich-history-john-t-thompson-of-newport-was-a-firearms-inventor-of-international-acclaim/.

O'Brien, Michael. "Tommy's Other Guns: Firearms Inventor John T. Thompson." Historynet, October 20, 2020. https://www.historynet.com/tommys-other-guns-firearms-inventor-john-t-thompson/.

Chapter 7: Thomas Hunt Morgan

Allen, Garland E. *Thomas Hunt Morgan: The Man and His Science*. Princeton, NJ: Princeton University Press, 1978.

Horowitz, Norman. "T.H. Morgan at Caltech: A Reminiscence." Genetics 149, no. 4 (August 1998): 1629–32.

Kandel, Eric. "Genes, Chromosomes, and the Origins of Modern Biology." *Columbia Magazine*, 1999. http://www.columbia.edu/cu/alumni/Magazine/Legacies/Morgan/.

Kean, Sam. *The Violinist's Thumb*. New York: Little, Brown and Co., 2012.

Keenan, Katherine. "Lilian Vaughan Morgan (1870–1952): Her Life and Work." *American Zoologist* 23, no. (1983): 867–76.

Chapter 8: Garrett Morgan

Blitz, Matt. "The Untold Story of the Man Who Called Himself the 'Black Edison.'" *Popular Mechanics*, September 13, 2016. https://www.popularmechanics.com/technology/design/a22802/garrett-morgan-inventor/.

DeLuca, Leo. "Black Inventor Garrett Morgan Saved Countless Lives with Gas Mask and Improved Traffic Lights." *Scientific American*, February 25, 2021. https://www.scientificamerican.com/article/black-inventor-garrett-morgan-saved-countless-lives-with-gas-mask-and-improved-traffic-lights/.

Chapter 9: St. Elmo Brady

American Chemical Society. "St. Elmo Brady." https://www.acs.org/content/acs/en/education/whatischemistry/landmarks/st-elmo-brady.html.
University of Illinois Department of Chemistry. https://chemistry.illinois.edu.
YouTube. "'Twenty Whites & One Other': St. Elmo Brady, First African-American Ph.D. in Chemistry." https://youtube.com/watch?v=lElk9iFlpCw.

Chapter 10: John Scopes

Fortune, Alonzo. "The Kentucky Campaign Against the Teaching of Evolution." *Journal of Religion* 2, no. 3 (May 1922): 225–35.
Moore, Randy. "The Long & Lingering Shadow of the Scopes Trial." *American Biology Teacher* 82, no. 2 (February 2020): 81–84
———. "What Scopes Told His Family & Friends About His Trial." *American Biology Teacher* 83, no. 2 (February 2021): 89–95.
Presley, James, and John T. Scopes. *Center of the Storm Memoirs of John T. Scopes.* New York: Holt, Rinehart and Winston, 1967.

Chapter 11: George Devol

Ballard, Leslie Anne, et. al. "George Charles Devol, Jr." *IEEE Robotics & Automation Magazine*, September 2012.
Malone, Bob. "George Devol: A Life Devoted to Invention, and Robots." IEEE Spectrum. https://spectrum.ieee.org/george-devol-a-life-devoted-to-invention-and-robots.
Munson, George. "The Rise and Fall of Unimation." Robot Magazine, September/October 2010.
Pearce, Jeremy. "George C. Devol, Inventor of Robot Arm, Dies at 99." *New York Times*, August 16, 2011. https://www.nytimes.com/2011/08/16/business/george-devol-developer-of-robot-arm-dies-at-99.html.

Williams, Hayley. "The Father of Modern Robotics: George Devol." Lifehacker, December 21, 2015. https://lifehacker.com.au/2015/12/the-father--of-modern-robotics-george-devol/.

Chapter 12: James Baker

National Academy of Engineering. *Memorial Tributes: Volume 11.* Washington, D.C.: The National Academies Press, 2007. https://doi.org/10.17226/11912.
Pearce, Jeremy. "J.G. Baker, Designer of High-Altitude Camera Lenses, Dies at 90." New York Times, July 13, 2005.

Chapter 13: William Lipscomb

Belmont Citizen-Herald. Mary Adele Lipscomb Obituary. September 25, 2007.
Lipscomb, James. "The Scientific Character of William N. Lipscomb, Jr." https://wlipscomb.tripod.com/.
Lipscomb, William N., Jr. Interview with Joanna Rose. December 3, 2001. https://www.nobelprize.org/prizes/chemistry/1976/lipscomb/25818-interview-transcript-1976/.
———. *Process of Discovery (1977); An Autobiographical Sketch.* Washington, D.C.: ACS Symposium Series, American Chemical Society, 2002.
Rees, Douglas C. *William N. Lipscomb, 1919–2011: A Biographical Memoir.* National Academy of Sciences, Washington, D.C.: National Academy of Sciences, 2019. www.nasonline.org/memoirs.

Chapter 14: William English

Hiltzik, Michael. "Column: Bill English, Wizard Behind the Scenes of Seminal Computer Technologies, Dies at 91." *Los Angeles Times,* July 31, 2020. https://www.latimes.com/business/story/2020-07-31/bill-english-dies-at-91.
Hintz, Eric. "The Mother of All Demos." National Museum of American History Smithsonian Institution, December 10, 2018. https://invention.si.edu/mother-all-demos.

Jordan, Ken. "The Click Heard Round the World." Wired, January 2004. https://www.wired.com/2004/01/mouse/.

Metz, Cade. "William English, Who Helped Build the Computer Mouse, Dies at 91." *New York Times*, July 31, 2020. https://www.nytimes.com/2020/07/31/technology/william-english-who-helped-build-the-computer-mouse-dies-at-91.html.

YouTube. "The Mother of All Demos, presented by Douglas Engelbart (1968)." https://youtube.com/watch?v=yJDv-zdhzMY&t=12s.

———. "White Rabbit: Interview with Doug Engelbart and Bill English, Moderated by John Markoff." December 13, 2013. https://www.youtube.com/watch?v=L1oNBImSXOM.

———. "Who Invented the Computer Mouse and Its Surprisingly Long Journey to Your Desk." September 8, 2017. https://www.youtube.com/watch?v=PdPN_QMjbCs&t=517s.

Chapter 15: George Whitesides

Arnaud, Celia Henry. "Always on the Move." *Chemical and Engineering News* 85, no. 13 (March 2007): 12–17. https://pubsapp.acs.org/cen/coverstory/85/8513cover1.html.

Whitesides, George M. *Curiosity and Science*. Angewandte Chemistry International Edition. 2018, 57, 2–6.

Chapter 16: Robert Grubbs

Bartleman, Bill. "Paducah's Nobel Prize Winner." *Paducah Sun*, October 6, 2005.

Nobel Prize. "Robert H. Grubbs Biographical." https://www.nobelprize.org/prizes/chemistry/2005/grubbs/biographical/.

Chapter 17: Phillip Sharp

Nobel Prize. "Phillip Sharps Biographical." https://www.nobelprize.org/prizes/medicine/1993/sharp/biographical.

YouTube. "Infinite History Project MIT: Phillip Sharp." https://www.youtube.com/watch?v=1hodN7hiO0&t=19s.

Chapter 18: Eugenia Wang

Chen, Ingfei. "The Accidental Biologist." *Science*, April 30, 2003. https://www.sciencemag.org/careers/2003/04/accidental-biologist.

PBS. "Dr. Eugenia Wang, Aging Research Expert." KET *One on One.* https://www.pbs.org/video/one-one-aging-research-expert-dr-eugenia-wang/.

Chapter 19: J. Richard Gott

Encyclopedia.com. "Gott, J. Richard, III 1947–." https://www.encyclopedia.com/arts/educational-magazines/gott-j-richard-iii-1947.

Neimark, Jill. "J. Richard Gott on Life, the Universe, and Everything." *Science & Spirit Magazine*, 2007. https://web.archive.org/web/20070928020457/http://www.science-spirit.org/article_detail.php?article_id=270.

Pearson Funeral Home. "Marjorie Gott." https://www.pearsonfuneralhome.com/obituaries/Marjorie-Gott/#!/Obituary.

Vanderkam, Laura. "Richard Gott: From Crystal Structures to Time Travel." *Scientific American*, March 2009. https://www.scientificamerican.com/article/richard-gott-westinghouse-time-travel/.

ABOUT THE AUTHOR

DUANE S. NICKELL was born and raised in Paducah, Kentucky. He is now a retired physics teacher living in Indianapolis with his wife, Karen Markman, and three cats. He holds a bachelor's degree from DePauw University, a master's degree from the University of Kentucky and a doctoral degree from Indiana University. He is a past president of the Hoosier Association of Science Teachers and a winner of the Presidential Award for Excellence in Science and Mathematics Teaching. His previous books include *Guidebook for the Scientific Traveler: Visiting Astronomy and Space Exploration Sites Across America*, *Guidebook for the Scientific Traveler: Visiting Physics and Chemistry Sites Across America* and *Scientific Indiana*. His author website is at www.duanenickell.com.

Visit us at
www.historypress.com